UFOs, ETs, and Alien Abductions

UFOs,
ETs, and
Alien Abductions

A Scientist Looks at the Evidence

Don Donderi, PhD

HAMPTON ROADS

Cover design by Jim Warner
Interior designed by Kathryn Sky-Peck

Hampton Roads Publishing Company, Inc.
Charlottesville, VA 22906
Distributed by Red Wheel/Weiser, LLC
www.redwheelweiser.com

Sign up for our newsletter and special offers by going to
www.redwheelweiser.com/newsletter/

Library of Congress Cataloging-in-Publication Data

Donderi, D. C.
    UFOs, ETs, and alien abductions : a scientist looks at the evidence /
Don Crosbie Donderi, PhD.
            pages cm
Includes bibliographical references and index.

ISBN 978-1-57174-695-5

    1. Unidentified flying objects--Sightings and encounters. 2. Extraterrestrial beings. 3. Alien abduction. I. Title. II. Title: Unidentified flying objects, extraterrestrials, and alien abductions.
TL789.D665 2013
001.942--dc23   2013000289

Printed on acid-free paper in United States of America

MAL

10 9 8 7 6 5 4 3 2 1

Dedicated to the memory of
Stuart Appelle and Budd Hopkins

Contents

Introduction

Human experience, which is constantly contradicting theory, is the great test of truth.

—Samuel Johnson

The Taconic State Parkway bisects the part of New York that lies to the east of the Hudson River from the New York City line almost as far north as Albany. During the first few months of 1983 people driving along the Parkway, on adjacent local roads and on nearby Interstate 84 saw low-flying objects covered with lights moving through the night sky. Looking past the lights they saw dark boomerang or triangle shapes the length and width of a football field, hovering just a few hundred feet above the ground. The objects moved at road traffic speed and then jumped from one place to another in the blink of an eye. Drivers slowed down, looked up, drove erratically, and pulled over and talked about what they were seeing. They reported the unidentified flying objects to local police. An officer who saw an object moving toward a nearby town would call that town's police, who would see the object moving on toward another town, and so on from town to town until the object blinked out or disappeared upward at tremendous speed. There were hundreds of reports like this in the Taconic State Parkway region and adjacent parts of New York and Connecticut from the end of 1982 through the middle of 1986.

The Federal Aviation Administration (FAA) said people were seeing "stunt pilots flying in formation." No one took that seriously.

When investigators asked about the sightings at the New York City FAA office, a secretary said "It is the policy of the FAA that UFOs do not exist, so we do not collect any reports of such."[1]

I met a professor of neuroscience from Rockefeller University in Manhattan who commuted to work on the Taconic State Parkway. He came to my university department to give a talk. At the reception after the talk I asked him whether he had seen one of the low-flying objects. He said he had. I asked him what he thought he had seen. He said the government had explained them so he hadn't bothered to think about it. His indifference to novelty staring him in the face is evidence that at least one scientist felt no curiosity about the world beyond his professional limits. His experience was not uncommon and neither was his scientist's reaction to the evidence before his eyes. Sightings like those along the Taconic State Parkway have happened many times over many years and in many places, and the scientific reaction to them has always been much the same.

Why I Study UFOs

My curiosity about UFOs, reinforced by professional training, motivated me to write this book. The humorist Dave Barry used the phrase "trained professional" as satirical shorthand for the unjustified confidence we sometimes place in experts. But I *am* a trained professional—a scientific specialist in what people see and remember (in professional language: human visual perception and memory), and my training is relevant to understanding the UFO phenomenon. On the basis of that training and my knowledge of the evidence, I think that some of what people report as UFOs are extraterrestrial vehicles. I think that some of those vehicles are like our unmanned reconnaissance drones, but others are crewed by extraterrestrials. I think that some people have come into involuntary close contact with extraterrestrials, and I think that government statements about UFOs conceal more than they reveal.

UFOs, ETs, and Alien Abductions summarizes the evidence about UFOs and close encounters. It explains why that evidence is reliable and why we react to it the way we do. It explains why most professional scientists ridicule or ignore the evidence. It argues that governments should reveal what they know about UFOs and close encounters. I have tried to meet a standard set by the American writer Tracy Kidder, who wrote that "the nonfiction writer's fundamental job is to make what is true believable."[2] My goal is to make the truth about extraterrestrial contact believable and to ask you to consider what it means for our future.

I started to read about UFOs when I was ten years old. I thought then that if people saw something in the sky, then there was probably something in the sky. If they said it wasn't an airplane or a kite or a rocket or a cloud or a planet, then it probably wasn't an airplane, a kite, a rocket, a cloud, or a planet. I am older now, and professionally trained, but I still believe that we know the world best through direct experience. When our senses turn up something new in the world, there *is* something new in the world, and it is an obligation of a trained professional who understands the human senses to report on it.

The next three cases describe something new in the world that I helped to report. These cases begin to explain why UFOs are real and why they are extraterrestrial; the rest of the book continues the story.

A Close Encounter in Quebec

The photograph in figure 1 on page xii was taken at Lake Baskatong in northern Quebec on March 11, 1978. Jim Smith and Bob Jones (not their real names), who lived near Montreal, drove to the lake, about 200 miles northwest of the city, to look at some shorefront property that Smith was thinking of buying. They left their car at a restaurant parking lot and then snowshoed several miles to the lake over an unplowed road, dragging a toboggan carrying their camping gear behind them. They were planning to stay overnight and return the next day. They set up camp and lit a fire. Smith went to gather more firewood when he saw a "bright star" moving slowly toward them. It dropped rapidly from the sky and hovered silently over the lake. He was carrying a camera and had the presence of mind to take four photos while Jones, who was also carrying a camera, stood transfixed. The UFO then moved off at an "unbelievable speed." Smith and Jones threw their gear onto the toboggan and started hiking back to their car. Smith turned to look behind him and saw the UFO again, now higher in the sky; seeing it was still there made them move even faster. They regained their car, stopped to rest and recover at the restaurant, and then drove straight home.

Figure 1. UFO photographed over Lake Baskatong, Quebec, Canada, by "Jim Smith" on March 11, 1978.

The photos were developed by Smith's brother-in-law, a professional photographer, then published in *The Montreal Star,* an English-language newspaper, and eventually in *Montréal,* a French-language magazine. Bill Wilson (not his real name), a Montreal engineer, saw the photos in the *Star.* He contacted Smith, who agreed to loan Wilson and me the original negatives. He also loaned us his camera and provided the photo development details.

During the summer of 1978 Wilson and Jim Smith and I drove to Lake Baskatong, found the spot from which the original photos had been taken, and using Smith's camera, took a series of test photos to compare to the originals.

I enlisted the help of a photo lab technician at my university to analyze the original and the test negatives using a Carl Zeiss III microscope system. While we watched, the technician viewed the original and test negatives under high magnification. He said the original negatives, which recorded the image of an immensely bright object, had not been tampered with. Based on the exposure details, image clarity, and the object's position relative to the trees and background in the original and test photos, we estimated that the object was about 1,000 feet from Smith and Jones.[3]

This observation is a *close encounter of the second kind* (CE-II), using terminology developed by J. Allen Hynek, a pioneer UFO researcher. A CE-II is an unidentified object seen at close range with physical evidence, in this case a photograph that permits further analysis.

A philosophical principle called Occam's razor tells us that if there is a choice among equally comprehensive explanations, the simplest explanation is best. In other words: don't complicate things unnecessarily. It certainly complicates things to explain the Smith-Jones observation and photographs as a record of an extraterrestrial vehicle, so we should ask how the razor-equipped skeptic would explain what they reported. The credibility of the story depends on the photographs; without the photographs the story is just words. Since the negatives were developed by the professional photographer brother-in-law, a simpler explanation, consistent with what we all know about human nature, is that the photographs are fakes and the story is a lie. This conclusion does not upset our understanding of the universe because while we have plenty of evidence about inconstant human nature, as skeptics we start with (at least taken one case at a time) little evidence about the existence of extraterrestrial vehicles. Much depends, then, on the credibility of the photographs.

The photographs are credible. Establishing their credibility also reassured the investigators about the character of Smith, who first tried to contact UFO-Québec, a UFO study group to which both Bill Wilson and I belonged, but was given a wrong telephone number. Smith then contacted *The Montreal Star*, which reported the sighting and published a picture of Smith holding prints of three of the four photos he had taken. When Bill Wilson finally contacted Smith, he had become disgusted with the persistent horde of reporters who descended on him after the *Star* story. Smith was now dubious about cooperating with UFO-Québec simply because he was a family man and had just learned firsthand the strain that unwanted publicity puts on normal life. Nevertheless, Smith loaned us the negatives and camera, his brother-in-law provided the development details, and the university photo technician confirmed by microscopic examination that the original negatives had not been altered.

If we accept that the photographs are real and the story is true, we still don't have to accept that the object was extraterrestrial. The simpler alternative is that it was man-made. But it wasn't a helicopter, for a couple of reasons: it made no sound, and it was intensely brilliant. While some helicopters are equipped with brilliant searchlights, they are not brilliant all over, and they are not shaped like the "flying saucer" photographed by Smith. If not a helicopter, it could have been a secret military craft that the average citizen knows nothing about. The hypothesis that Smith photographed a secret military craft is an alternative to the hypothesis that he photographed an extraterrestrial vehicle. The rest of this book is an extended argument that the most likely explanation for Smith and Jones's photographically recorded close encounter with a UFO, and many other similar reports, is that extraterrestrial vehicles exist.

Humanoids

On a summer night in 1973 Professor X was driving east toward Montreal on a road near the Ottawa River. His wife and son were also in the car. Mrs. X, who was sitting in the front passenger seat, saw a light some distance away to the left of the road. She mentioned it to her husband. He paid no attention so she continued to watch

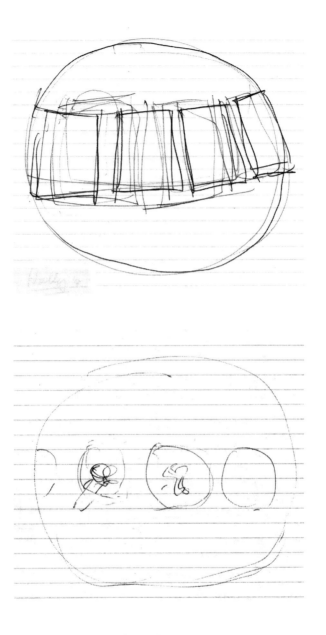

Figure 2. Drawings by Professor X (bottom) and Mrs. X (top) of their close encounter with a UFO along the Ottawa River in Canada during the summer of 1973.

it silently. At first she thought it was a star, but it seemed to be too close to the ground. It looked like it was moving. Knowing it was the summer of the comet Kohoutek, she thought that she might be watching the comet. By now the light had been in view for more than an hour, pacing them as they drove past the city of Ottawa in the deepening twilight. She kept seeing it across open fields to the left of the car. It was no longer just a point of light, but appeared to be rounded, and for a moment—despite the fact that it had been following them—she thought that it looked like an illuminated, spherical water tower. The sky was now completely dark, and as the object approached the road she could see that there was nothing under it holding it up. The object paced their car. Suddenly windows opened on the object's rounded surface and bright light shone toward them. Professor X saw human-like figures moving behind the windows as the sphere passed over them and then moved away, behind the car. They remembered the sighting lasting about ten seconds from the time the UFO paced them alongside the road to the time it passed out of sight behind the car. Mrs. X corroborated the UFO details, including the windows, but she does not remember seeing figures. Their son was asleep in the backseat.

Several years later, Professor X and I had administrative jobs that brought us into regular contact at my university. My interest in UFOs was known at the university, and Professor X's attitude was skeptical. He never volunteered a word about his own experience.

Bill Wilson, who investigated the Lake Baskatong case with me, is an engineer whose travels take him to many cities across Canada and abroad. When in Ottawa, Canada's capital, he used to visit the National Research Council (NRC), the agency that administers scientific research on behalf of the Canadian government. In the 1970s the government was under public and parliamentary pressure to "do something" about the scores of UFOs that were reported to the Royal Canadian Mounted Police (RCMP) from military, provincial, and local police observers as well as private citizens. In response, the NRC set up the Non-meteorite Sighting File, which contained reports of aerial phenomena that were puzzles to NRCs own experts;

observations that could not be explained as atmospheric phenomena, ball lightning, or meteorites. The Non-meteorite Sighting File was open to the public so long as readers promised not to reveal the names of witnesses.

Mrs. X wrote a letter to the NRC describing what they had seen, and NRC filed it in the Non-meteorite Sighting File. Because she had written a personal letter they wrote her a personal reply. They told Mrs. X that she and her husband had seen a DC-9 in the landing pattern for the Ottawa Airport. Mrs. X had not bothered to tell the NRC that her husband, a PhD scientist and university administrator, was also a Royal Canadian Air Force pilot (in the reserves), had flown multiengine military aircraft for many years, and knew where a DC-9 in a landing pattern at Ottawa airport would be and what it would look like. What Professor and Mrs. X saw was not a DC-9 in the landing pattern for the Ottawa airport. It was a UFO at close range, and one of the witnesses saw humanoids behind the windows.

Bill Wilson found Mrs. X's letter in the Non-meteorite Sighting File on one of his visits to the NRC. Mrs. X had mentioned what her husband did for a living, so Bill knew that I could contact her husband and find out more about the sighting (despite the nondisclosure rule!). Bill called me and told me who had written the letter, not knowing that Professor X and I already knew each other. The next time I saw Professor X, I mentioned the letter. He was embarrassed, but only briefly. He invited my wife and me to dinner the following week, and after dinner he and his wife told us the story that you have just read, with agitation and emotion.

Now, many years later, I still run into Professor X occasionally. We have not spoken about their close encounter again. It is unlikely that the Xs will mention their story to anyone else. Establishment scientists and their wives do not talk about UFO close encounters over cocktails at the Faculty Club. There may be more to this event than an hour or more of pacing by a UFO followed by a ten-second close encounter, but, as far as I know, neither Professor X nor his wife or son have any interest in finding out. However, I am grateful to them for having told us about it, and that is where this story ends.

Abductions

The late Budd Hopkins was a painter and sculptor whose interest in UFOs began with his own daylight sighting in 1964 and was reinforced when he investigated a New York City neighbor's close encounter in 1975.[4] Many of the people he later interviewed said they had been taken aboard a UFO. Hopkins asked these people who had experienced a so-called "alien abduction" to draw any symbols that they remembered having seen aboard the craft during the experience.

Hopkins saved drawings made by twenty-four people who said they could remember symbols. The late Stuart Appelle, an experimental psychologist like me and also the editor of the *Journal of UFO Studies*, realized that he could compare the drawings made by Hopkins' abductees with drawings made by people who never claimed to have been abducted by aliens. Appelle hypnotized twenty-four non-abducted "control subjects" and asked them under hypnosis to *imagine* being taken aboard a UFO. When they had regained normal consciousness after the hypnosis Appelle asked them to draw any symbols they remembered seeing inside the craft during their hypnotically suggested "abduction." If the symbols remembered by Hopkins' abductees matched the symbols "remembered" by Appelle's hypnotized imaginary abductees, that would suggest the whole alien abduction experience was also imaginary.

I had developed a statistical method that allowed unbiased observers to decide in what ways each of the forty-eight drawings were alike or different.[5] If the Hopkins drawings and the imaginary Appelle drawings were mixed up by the impartial observers, then the Hopkins drawings—and the experience that produced them— could also be considered imaginary. But if the two sets of drawings were judged by impartial observers to be different, then Hopkins' abductees would have memories that were *(1)* internally consistent, and *(2)* consistently different from the memories of people who had only imagined that they had been abducted.

APPELLE IMAGES   **HOPKINS IMAGES**

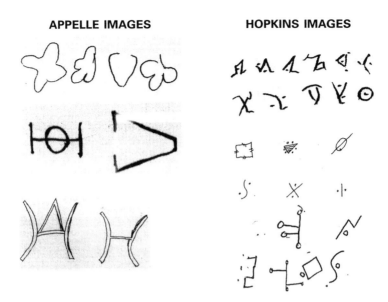

Figure 3. Symbols drawn by Stuart Appelle's hypnotized imaginary abductees (left), and Hopkins' self-reported abductees (right).

The result of the experiment was clear: the original Hopkins drawings and Appelle's imaginary drawings were different.[6] Figure 3 shows some of the Hopkins drawings as well as some of the drawings made by people who were hypnotized and asked to "remember" symbols they saw inside a UFO. The Hopkins symbols were unique; whatever produced them was not the work of pure imagination. This symbol evidence is consistent with, but not sufficient proof of, the conclusion that the abduction experiences were real.

Witnesses, Investigators, and Evidence

I met the witnesses in the Lake Baskatong case, I know the witnesses in the Professor X case, and I met some of the witnesses who provided abductee symbols to Budd Hopkins. Nothing in the behavior or personal history of any of them leads me to think that they are mentally disturbed or that they told fabulous stories for personal or psychological gain. When visual perception and memory produce accounts like theirs, it should be clear why their cases are interesting to someone whose business is the study of human visual perception and memory. I have not participated as directly in collecting the rest of the evidence presented in this book; it has been gathered by many competent people over many years. What follows is a consistent story reported by competent witnesses and evaluated by competent investigators. It begins, in the next chapter, with the modern history of UFOs.

PART ONE

UFOs

Pure logical thinking cannot yield us any knowledge of the empirical world; all knowledge of reality starts from experience and ends in it.

—Albert Einstein

1

UFOs and the Cold War

U FOs first came to the attention of the American public in 1947, during the long Cold War between the Western Allies and the Soviet Union that started in 1945 and lasted until the Soviet Union collapsed in 1991. The next three chapters outline the UFO evidence along with the controversies and arguments among government spokesmen, scientists, and media that accompanied all public discussion of UFOs during that time. This sets the stage for later chapters that describe the extraterrestrials, report on contacts between extraterrestrials and us, outline the scientific reaction to the UFO phenomenon, and review the social and political consequences of our interaction with extraterrestrial civilization.

The Index Case: Kenneth Arnold

The first officially recorded case of an epidemic is called the *index case.*[7] The index case for the modern UFO "epidemic" was the 1947 Kenneth Arnold sighting. If it had been an isolated event it would have dropped off the front pages and out of history, but it was the first of many reported sightings of UFOs in 1947 and throughout the late 1940s and the 1950s.

Arnold, a private pilot, was a self-employed businessman who sold fire-suppression equipment throughout the American Northwest. On June 24, 1947, he had installed some equipment in Chehalis,

Washington, when he was told that a military transport plane was missing and presumed lost in the Cascade Mountains. On his return flight east from Chehalis across the Cascades he decided to look for the missing plane and changed his flight plan to fly closer to Mount Rainier. As he was making a turn a flash of light caught his eye. He thought it was a reflection from a nearby airplane and looked for it, but he saw only an airliner far away to his left and behind him. A second flash caught his eye. This time he saw it was reflected from a formation of nine bright objects traveling south between Mount Baker, far to his north, and Mount Rainier, closer to the north on his left. They were flying in echelon formation with the lead object highest as they passed over Mount Rainier and flew south ahead of his course. They disappeared over Mount Adams to the south. Knowing the distance between the mountain peaks, he estimated their speed at more than 1,200 miles per hour—faster than the few new jet planes of the era. He landed at Yakima, Washington and mentioned the sighting to people he knew at the airport, saying he had no idea what he had seen. Figure 4 shows Arnold's drawing of what he saw. His listeners suggested that he had seen guided missiles.

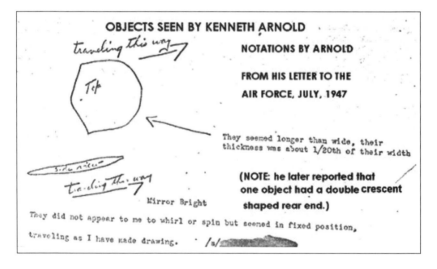

Figure 4. Kenneth Arnold's drawing of one of the UFOs he saw over the Cascade Mountains in Washington State on June 24, 1947.

From Yakima Arnold flew on to Pendleton, Oregon, where an air show was about to start. Word of his sighting had preceded him, and when he landed he faced a crowd of interested air show spectators. One person he met there had also seen the same or similar "mystery missiles" on the same day, and the consensus was again that Arnold had seen guided missiles.

Arnold talked to a reporter from the *East Oregonian* newspaper about the objects, but he did not suggest that they were extraterrestrial. He remarked to the reporter that the objects' flight reminded him of a flat rock bouncing as it skipped across water. The "flying saucer" tag came neither from Arnold nor from the newspaper account, but was created by an anonymous writer who headlined the story circulated by the Associated Press.

The Arnold story triggered reports of about twenty similar sightings on June 24th, almost all of them in the Northwest. A prospector who had been working in the Cascades that day said he had watched "round, metallic-looking discs" maneuvering overhead. He counted "five or six" but added that he was looking at one of them through his telescope and may have missed seeing the rest. During the last week of June and all of July so many reports came in that fighters were sent up on "saucer patrol" in the Northwest. An Air National Guard pilot from North Dakota chased a disk but could not catch it.[8]

Skeptics, who by and large are reasonable people, and debunkers, who are dedicated non-believers with no sense of humor, have been trying to explain away the Arnold sighting ever since it happened. Consider misleading mischief as an explanation. Nothing in Arnold's life as a businessman and flyer suggests that mischief is the explanation. What would he have to gain? He never claimed that what he saw was extraterrestrial; just that it was unique. He did become a mild celebrity in the UFO field as a result of his encounter, and he wrote a book and some articles about his experience, but it never became a major part of his life, and he continued his fire-suppression business long after the 1947 sighting.

An alternative suggestion is that Arnold may have seen some natural phenomenon. The two phenomena suggested were snow blowing off the mountain peaks and lenticular clouds forming over the mountains. Arnold had been flying around mountains for years, and he would have seen snow blowing off the peaks and lenticular clouds many times before. There is no reason to think that his memory suddenly failed him on June 24, 1947.

The debunker Donald Menzel gave three different explanations of Arnold's sighting in three different books, the last explanation being that he had seen raindrops on his window. Menzel ignored Arnold's statement that he had lowered his side window to better see the objects. And what about the option first suggested to Arnold: guided missiles? In 1947 no country in the world could fly anything faster than 1,200 miles per hour and maneuver it around a range of mountain peaks.

The newspaper accounts about the sightings in the Northwest gave little credence to the possibility of extraterrestrial origin. While the papers acknowledged that the sightings were mysterious, other explanations predominated. Either the UFOs were misperceptions, or hallucinations, or military technology—American or foreign. World War II had been succeeded by the Cold War, which influenced both public and government responses to the new UFOs.

The RB-47 Case

On the night of July 17, 1957, a UFO stalked a US Air Force RB-47 electronic reconnaissance plane for one and a half hours over an 800-mile course from the Mississippi Gulf Coast to Oklahoma. The RB-47 tried to catch the UFO twice, but it was outrun or outmaneuvered both times. The UFO was seen by the crew, detected by the RB-47's sensors, and tracked by a ground radar station that painted the RB-47 and the UFO at the same time.

The UFO appeared first as an invisible radar source that was tracked by the RB-47's airborne radar receivers. The invisible source appeared to follow and then circle the RB-47 as it flew over

Gulfport, Mississippi. As the aircraft flew further inland, the radar source suddenly appeared to the crew as a "very intense white light with [a] light blue tint" that flashed across the airplane's flight path and took up a position to the right side of the aircraft before it blinked out. The radar-emitting source moved with the light, and even after the light blinked out, the radar source never disappeared from the RB-47's radar receivers. The "huge light" then reappeared at the same bearing as the radar source and below the RB-47.

The RB-47 captain asked for and got permission from air traffic control to deviate from his flight plan and chase the radar-emitting light. He went to full power and dived, but as the RB-47 gained the object suddenly stopped in mid-air below him and the RB-47 overshot it. He turned back toward the object, but when the RB-47 got within five nautical miles the UFO dropped lower and both the RB-47 and the ground radar station lost contact with it. Running low on fuel because of the extended high-speed chase, the captain radioed the ground station that he had to set a course for home (Topeka, Kansas), at which point the object then took up station behind the RB-47 and was again recorded on the airplane's radar receivers until the RB-47 had passed Oklahoma City on its way home, when the radar signal finally faded out.

This case has an official pedigree because it was assembled from flight plans, mission reports, and communications transcripts that were retained as military records.[9] There can be no doubt about witness reliability because the six aircraft crew members plus the ground-based radar tracking and flight control reporters were all either military personnel or government employees whose careers depended, at the very least, on bureaucratic punctiliousness. Separate follow-up phone interviews with the six flight crewmembers were also consistent.

About ten years after the Kenneth Arnold index case there is reliable evidence that a fast, maneuverable object seen visually and reported on radar stalked and outmaneuvered a frontline US military aircraft. The malfeasance or misperception explanation cannot explain this case. Three alternative explanations are that the visual and radar observations were: a previously unknown atmospheric-meteorological event, a secret military craft not known to the airmen and radar operators, or an extraterrestrial vehicle. The atmospheric-meteorological explanation is weakened by the fact that no one knows how the atmosphere and the weather could produce such an effect. The secret military explanation is weakened by two arguments: first, it wasn't "secret" if it was playing tag with a frontline military air-craft where it could both be seen and tracked on radar; and second, no terrestrial machine an entire half-century after this event can even approximate its performance. That leaves the third explanation: the object was an extraterrestrial vehicle.

The Coyne Helicopter Incident

An Army Reserve helicopter nearly collided with a UFO over central Ohio on the night of October 18, 1973. The four-man crew, commanded by Reserve Lieutenant Lawrence Coyne, flew their UH-1 "Huey" medevac helicopter 125 miles southwest from Cleveland to Columbus, Ohio, to complete routine medical checkups. As they returned to Cleveland that night it was clear and the helicopter was flying at 1,700 feet above rolling terrain. At about 11:00 p.m., over Mansfield, Ohio, one of the crew noticed a red light on the southeast horizon and told Coyne, who said "keep an eye on it." A few seconds later the crewmember said the light was moving toward them on a collision course. Coyne put the UH-1 into a 500-feet-per-minute descent. He called the Mansfield control tower to check on nearby traffic but got no response (a follow-up found no other civil or military airplanes in the area). The red light kept approaching, and Coyne kept the ship in a descent until they had just about reached the ground—about 650 feet up. As the object reached the UH-1, it stopped and hovered above and in front of the helicopter. A cigar-shaped, domed object almost filled the front windshield. It had a red light at the bow, a white light at the stern, and a movable beam that swung from the bottom of the

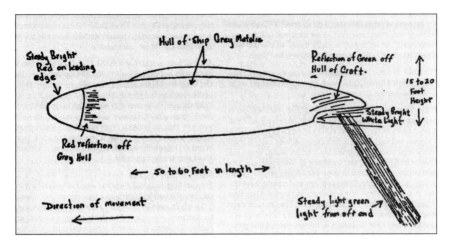

Figure 5. Sketch of the UFO that intercepted a US Army helicopter over Ohio in October 1973.

object over the nose of the helicopter and into the cockpit, filling it with green light. Figure 5 is a drawing of what Coyne and his crew saw. The object stayed over the helicopter for an estimated ten seconds and then sped off to the west and eventually out of sight to the north in the direction of Lake Erie. As the object left, the helicopter's magnetic compass swung wildly and the UH-1 climbed to an altitude of 3,500 feet even though Coyne was still holding the control lever for descent.

Nearby, a family of four was driving on the road below. They saw a red and a green light descend rapidly toward their car and they stopped and got out of the car to look at it, when they also heard and then saw the helicopter approaching from the south. They then saw the red-and-green lighted object, which they said looked like a blimp and was as big as a school bus, hovering over the helicopter. The green light suddenly got brighter and lit up the helicopter as well as the family on the ground beneath, who, now thoroughly frightened, scrambled back into their car and drove off.

Was this a misperception or a hoax? Military officers and flight crew who want to keep their jobs do not report hoaxes. The independent ground witnesses and the flight report filed by Lieutenant Coyne agree about the details of the encounter. All four helicopter witnesses agree both about what they saw and about their maneuvers before and after the encounter. There was a physical effect: the helicopter's magnetic compass failed immediately after the encounter and had to be replaced.

Was the UFO a secret military or civil aircraft? Only if the United States or a foreign power was testing a secret aircraft over Ohio in the middle of the night and while doing so, dangerously interfering with a routine military helicopter flight. It was seen at close range and was not recognized by any of the witnesses as a military or civil aircraft. Its performance was extraordinary. Forty years later, no existing aircraft can do what that UFO did.

The 1948 Air Force Estimate of the Situation

A military intelligence report is called an "estimate of the situation." The Estimate of the Situation written in the summer of 1948 by members of the UFO investigation group Project Sign, part of the US Air Force Air Technical Intelligence Center (ATIC), was particularly significant. You have just read three UFO reports more or less as they were communicated to readers when they were first written. What is your estimate of the situation? You should say: "Based on what I have read, it's far too early to tell." But imagine that over the past year you have received more than two hundred reports like the three you have just read; most from military personnel on duty, many from pilots in the air and radar and control tower operators on the ground. The ATIC Estimate of the Situation concluded that UFOs were probably extraterrestrial. The report with its extraterrestrial hypothesis (ETH) was rejected by the Air Force Chief of Staff, who ordered it destroyed. But the report and its conclusions became known through leaks to civilian investigators and a book written by former Air Force officer Edward J. Ruppelt.[10]

The current US Air Force estimate of the situation states:

- No UFO reported, investigated, and evaluated by the Air Force was ever an indication of threat to our national security.

- There was no evidence submitted to or discovered by the Air Force that sightings categorized as Unidentified represented technological developments or principles beyond the range of modern scientific knowledge; and

- There was no evidence indicating that sightings categorized as Unidentified were extraterrestrial vehicles.[11]

The Air Force statement is a succinct and convenient summary of everything I intend to disprove. Discounting the reports that are explainable as hoaxes, misperceptions of natural phenomena, or human artifacts, my goal is to demonstrate that many UFO reports describe machines that are technologically superior to anything humans can now produce. These machines are extraterrestrial vehicles, and they are a threat to national security because we cannot defend against them. I will explain why more than sixty years of evidence in support of the ETH has been ignored or dismissed by almost everyone who holds a position of responsibility or trust in government and science. The truth of the ETH will become self-evident to any intelligent person who learns the facts.

From 1947 to about 1980, UFO history could be described as a "chronology of doubt." The doubt resulted from the interaction of the UFO evidence with the goals and personalities of the people and organizations responding to that evidence. This includes the press and television, UFO witnesses, charlatans, local police forces, the US Air Force, the Central Intelligence Agency (CIA), scientists associated with the Air Force and the CIA, and the founders and members of UFO interest groups. The chronology is outlined in figures 6a and 6b on pages 12 and 13.

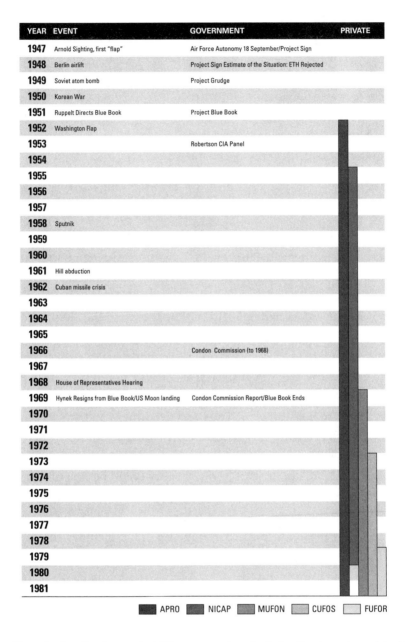

YEAR	EVENT	GOVERNMENT	PRIVATE
1947	Arnold Sighting, first "flap"	Air Force Autonomy 18 September/Project Sign	
1948	Berlin airlift	Project Sign Estimate of the Situation: ETH Rejected	
1949	Soviet atom bomb	Project Grudge	
1950	Korean War		
1951	Ruppelt Directs Blue Book	Project Blue Book	
1952	Washington Flap		
1953		Robertson CIA Panel	
1954			
1955			
1956			
1957			
1958	Sputnik		
1959			
1960			
1961	Hill abduction		
1962	Cuban missile crisis		
1963			
1964			
1965			
1966		Condon Commission (to 1968)	
1967			
1968	House of Representatives Hearing		
1969	Hynek Resigns from Blue Book/US Moon landing	Condon Commission Report/Blue Book Ends	
1970			
1971			
1972			
1973			
1974			
1975			
1976			
1977			
1978			
1979			
1980			
1981			

APRO NICAP MUFON CUFOS FUFOR

Figure 6a. Timeline for events, UFO groups, and media during the chronology of doubt.

UFOs, ETs, and Alien Abductions

BOOKS AND MEDIA	SIGHTINGS		
1947	Jan-47	38	
1948	May-48	10	
1949	Apr-49	16	
1950	Jan-50	28	
The Day the Earth Stood Still (movie)	Jan-51	23	
1952	Jan-52	52	
Keyhoe: *Flying Saucers from Outer Space* /Menzel: *Flying Saucers*	Jan-53	35	
1954	Jan-54	53	
1955	Feb-55	37	
Ruppelt, *Report on Unidentified Flying Objects* (2 editions)	Jan-56	40	
1957	Jan-57	72	
1958	Jan-58	45	
1959	Jan-59	49	
1960	Jan-60	66	
1961	Jan-61	44	
1962	Jan-62	60	
1963	Jan-63	79	
NICAP: *The UFO Evidence*	Jan-64	82	
Fuller: *Incident at Exeter*	Jan-65	175	
Fuller: *Interrupted Journey*	Jan-66	185	
1967	Jan-67	191	
Klass: *UFOs Identified*/Congressional Symposium on UFOs	Jan-68	207	
1969	Jan-69	152	
1970	Jan-70	138	
1971	Jan-71	125	
Hynek: *UFOs a Scientific Inquiry*	Jan-72	166	
1973	Jan-73	215	
1974	Jan-74	260	
Klass: *UFOs Explained* /Jacobs: *UFO Controversy in America*	Jan-75	303	
1976	Jan-76	269	
Close Encounters of the Third Kind (movie)	Jan-77	247	
1978	Jan-78	335	
1979	Jan-79	241	
1980	Jan-80	233	
Hopkins: *Missing Time*	Jan-81	152	

Figure 6b. Timeline for sightings during the chronology of doubt.

After the Arnold Sighting

The US Air Force, formerly the US Army Air Force, became an independent military service on September 18, 1947—three months after the Kenneth Arnold sighting. UFO reports became the Air Force's business because it was responsible for the air defense of the United States. Reports were sent to the ATIC at Wright-Patterson Air Force Base near Dayton, Ohio, which collected information about all foreign aviation technology. ATIC first thought UFOs were Soviet weapons developed by captured German scientists. During the Second World War, Germany had designed disc-shaped flying objects, the so-called "Horten discs," so the military and civilian technologists at ATIC assumed that further Soviet development of the German discs might be responsible for the UFO sightings, and they scrambled to learn as much as possible about them. But it turned out that the Soviets had not captured the appropriate German technology; nor, for that matter, had they captured the appropriate Germans.

The US Navy had tested an experimental aircraft nicknamed the "Flying Pancake," which had a thin, disc-like profile, but by the time of the Arnold sighting the project had been canceled and the one test aircraft was in a museum. ATIC officers contacted every other American research and development group that could have been developing something like a UFO, but they came up empty.

In December 1947, the ad hoc UFO investigation within ATIC became Project Sign. Within Project Sign, opinion about the origin of UFOs was divided. The possibilities were: Soviet technology (weakened by the failure to find supporting evidence in Europe); US technology (weakened by the failure to find an American UFO source); human error, in the form of hoaxes or misperceptions of meteors, planets, stars, or aircraft landing lights; or, finally, extraterrestrial vehicles. Project opinion was biased toward either the Soviet or the extraterrestrial option, while public opinion, as assessed through Gallup Polls, favored either US technology or human error.[12]

High-ranking Air Force officers disagreed about the Project Sign Estimate of the Situation. The pro-UFO faction thought the ETH was tenable, if not proven. The anti-UFO faction thought the ETH was false and dangerous because publicity about "flying saucers" would make people anxious about Soviet military power and would sap confidence in the value of the American monopoly of the atomic bomb (in 1948). The anti-UFO faction won, and the Estimate was rejected by the Air Force. The ATIC Project Sign was renamed Project Grudge in February 1949. ATIC officers who wrote the Estimate of the Situation were transferred elsewhere. The between-the-lines message from the Pentagon to the new project management was that the *UFO phenomenon*, not the UFO, was a danger to national security. Project Grudge's job was to explain away the UFO phenomenon in order to reduce public anxiety about extraterrestrials and Soviet secret weapons.[13]

A Sketch of the Cold War

A sketch of some major world events from 1939 to 1953 explains, if it does not excuse, why UFO evidence was treated as it was by the Air Force. World War II against Germany began in Europe in September 1939 and ended with victory for the Western Allies in May 1945. World War II began for United States against both Germany and Japan on December 7, 1941, with the Japanese attack on Pearl Harbor and continued until the United States exploded atomic bombs over Hiroshima on August 6 and Nagasaki on August 9, 1945, forcing the Japanese government to surrender on August 14.

By the end of the war the armies of the Soviet Union had driven the German army out of much of Austria, the Baltic States, Bulgaria, Czechoslovakia, Hungary, Poland, Rumania, and Yugoslavia and had occupied about one-half of Germany, including Berlin. Soviet forces entered the Pacific War against Japan at the last minute, invading and occupying the northern half of the Korean Peninsula, where they established a Communist government. The American and British Commonwealth Allies had regained the rest of continental Europe and the parts of Africa lost to the Axis powers. Spain, Portugal, and Sweden had been neutral, and Finland had settled its armed quarrel with the Soviet Union earlier.

The Western Allies disarmed in 1945 but the Soviet Union did not. Soviet commissars backed by Soviet armies forced Soviet-style governments on all of Eastern Europe plus their half of a divided Germany. The Soviets encouraged a Communist insurgency in Greece, which was defeated with British and American financial and military support. The Soviets quit their occupation zone of Austria in 1955, but Soviet-supported Communist parties worked to subvert other non-Communist governments in Europe. Communist political influence was strong in Italy and France and was overcome partly through American money and influence. As the sole occupying power, the United States reformed the Japanese government and economy, redistributed land, and established representative government before returning the country to Japanese rule in 1952.

In June 1948 the Soviets denied the Western Allies road access from Allied-controlled West Germany through Soviet-controlled territory in East Germany to Berlin, which was then jointly occupied by Britain, France, the United States, and the Soviet Union. In response the Allies set up the Berlin Airlift which kept the city supplied with food and coal through the summer of 1948 and the winter of 1948–1949. The Soviets withdrew the blockade and the Allies stayed in Berlin.

Aided by spies in Los Alamos, New Mexico, where the American atomic bomb had been designed and built, the Soviet Union exploded its first atomic bomb in August of 1949. This was years before Western scientists expected the Soviets to break the American monopoly on the bomb. The Soviet atomic bomb, combined with Communist domination of eastern and central Europe, Communist insurgency and subversion in other Western democracies and the lesson of the Berlin Airlift persuaded America and its allies to rearm and establish the North Atlantic Treaty Organization (NATO) in 1949 as a defense against the Soviet threat. American rearmament included increased strategic bombing capability and stronger air defenses—both responsibilities of the US Air Force.

On June 25, 1950, Communist North Korea attacked South Korea. Within weeks the North Koreans overran most of South Korea except a beachhead around the southern port city of Busan, held by the South Koreans with the help of American troops rushed in from the occupation forces in Japan. The Soviet Union made a political error by boycotting a UN Security Council meeting, and the UN passed a resolution condemning the invasion and calling on other governments to support the South Koreans. A surprise American amphibious landing at Incheon, near South Korea's capital, Seoul, returned the initiative to the Allies who surged through North Korea all the way to the Yalu River, the border with Communist China. The Allies were driven back by Chinese Communist troops to roughly the 38th parallel, the prewar boundary between the two Koreas. An armistice in 1953 brought the fighting to a halt, but there is no peace treaty and the status quo is an armed standoff.

Nikita Khrushchev, the then first secretary of the Communist Party of the Soviet Union, uttered his famous "We will bury you!" threat to the West in 1956, but Western leaders believed that Joseph Stalin, the former dictator of the Soviet Union, already had that in mind.

The motivation for this Cold War sketch is to show why the unanticipated and unwanted appearance of unidentified flying objects in 1947 was a distraction from the Air Force's immediate task of defending the United States against an enemy bent on spreading international communism by subversion or by war.

Contactees

As UFO evidence began to accumulate, a half-dozen or so energetic charlatans proclaimed that they had already been in contact with the extraterrestrials. Following an old American tradition, each established his own quasi religion centered on the contactee himself, who transmitted reassuring and prophetic messages from the space beings. The contactees wrote books and articles, held meetings, organized associations with local chapters, and held conventions where "believers" gathered together and absorbed the messages and encouragement that the Space Brothers conveyed to their chosen representatives on Earth.[14]

The contactees were a colorful but disruptive addition to the chronology of doubt. "Professor" George Adamski wrote *Flying Saucers Have Landed* in 1953. He communicated with the Master and learned that Jesus was one of the Space Brothers' earlier emissaries to Earth. Truman Bethurum wrote *Aboard a Flying Saucer* in 1954 and socialized with Aura Rhanes, a beauty who lived on the planet Clarion on the same orbit as Earth but on the opposite side of the sun. "Dr." Daniel Fry, who wrote *The White Sands Incident* in 1954, was driven here and there in spaceships and communicated with Alan, who told him to warn Earth about the dangers of nuclear war. Orfeo Angelucci wrote *The Secret of the Saucers* in 1955, describing a saucer ride with the beautiful Lyra. Howard Menger wrote *From Outer Space to You* in 1959; he met and married the beautiful spacewoman Marla. George Van Tassel owned desert property at the Giant Rock in the Yucca Valley, east of Los Angeles. He ran the Giant Rock Convention every year from 1954 to 1978 as a gathering place for contactees and their followers. Five thousand people showed up to the first convention.

From 1947 through 1980 contactees were as noticeable as the UFO evidence itself. In 1978 I gave a talk about UFOs to a Montreal audience. As I entered the room twenty minutes before the talk, a woman at the door was passing out literature about the Spirit of Light from the Space Brothers, by whose rules we must all learn to live. All I could do at the start of my talk was to dissociate myself from the contactee at the door.

Edward J. Ruppelt and Project Blue Book

Edward J. Ruppelt was a B-29 bombardier who returned to college after World War II and earned an aeronautical engineering degree. He took over ATIC's UFO investigation after he was recalled to active duty in 1951 during the Korean War. Ruppelt left the Air Force in 1953 after his UFO stint and went to work for Northrop Grumman as an engineer, but died of a heart attack in 1960 at the early age of thirty-seven.

Ruppelt wrote *The Report on Unidentified Flying Objects* about his UFO investigations from 1951 to 1953, first as the officer assigned to reactivate Project Grudge and then as the officer in charge when Project Grudge was renamed Project Blue Book. The first edition of his book was published in 1956. The last chapter, called "What Are UFOs?", ended like this: "Maybe the earth is being visited by interplanetary spaceships. Only time will tell." The first edition is a readable, humorous, and intelligent account of Ruppelt's capable response to an elusive phenomenon within a conflicted bureaucracy. The last chapter of the second edition, published in 1960, was called "Do They or Don't They?" and ended like this: "No responsible scientist will argue with the fact that other solar systems may be inhabited and that some day we may meet those people. But it hasn't happened yet and until that day comes we're stuck with our Space Age myth: the UFO."

The second edition includes cases that occurred after Ruppelt left the Air Force. It winds down with *identified* sightings; for example, a weather balloon mistakenly called an Unknown. It supports the implication consistent with the current Air Force position that there will always be few "UFOs," but that they all could be identified as natural phenomena or human artifacts if we only had more information. Although Ruppelt changed his interpretation of UFO history between the first and the second editions, the first edition is an informative account of both the phenomenon and the Air Force response as it evolved during the late 1940s and early '50s. Ruppelt was as close to his sources as the Greek historian Thucydides, who wrote *History of the Peloponnesian War*:

> And with reference to the narrative of events, . . . I did not even trust my own impressions, but it rests partly on what I saw myself, partly on what others saw for me, the accuracy of the report being always tried by the most severe and detailed tests possible.[15]

Project Grudge to Blue Book

When Ruppelt rejoined the Air Force he was sent to ATIC to analyze the performance of the Russian MiG-15 jet fighter that American pilots were facing in Korea. UFO reports were still arriving at the moribund Project Grudge. Ruppelt's desk was near the Project Grudge desk and now and then he would look over some of the UFO reports. The Grudge message in 1951 was that UFOs were either outright misperceptions or would be classified as misperceptions if more information were available.

In September 1951 the Grudge message fell apart. Reports of a series of radar observations and visual UFO sightings went both to Project Grudge and to the Pentagon, where the Air Force director of Intelligence, not a member of the anti-UFO faction, asked for more details from ATIC. ATIC sent two officers to interview some of the military witnesses, and they then flew directly to Washington to brief the brass. One of the interviewing officers was a competent young engineer recalled to active service and then assigned to Project Grudge. He "told it like it was" to a large meeting of Pentagon intelligence officers. Top brass was incensed that the project was moribund within ATIC, and the intelligence chief immediately ordered the competent young officer to revitalize it.

The competent young officer had just begun to get things moving when he was released from military service to return to his defense-related engineering project at Caltech. Knowing that Ruppelt, who was still in the Air Force, was also a competent engineer, the chief of

UFOs, ETs, and Alien Abductions

ATIC's aircrafts and missiles branch asked Ruppelt to take over Project Grudge, which he did. Ruppelt had access to all of Project Sign and Project Grudge's poorly archived records, which he and his staff of ten reorganized. From 1951 through much of 1953 he was responsible for the analysis of all military (including Army and Navy) UFO reports. Regulations made it mandatory for all UFO sightings and observations to be directly reported to him by intelligence officers at every Air Force base, and he had *carte blanche* to visit Air Force bases to follow up on cases. After Ruppelt took over, the project got a new name—Project Blue Book.

Project Grudge/Blue Book Under Ruppelt

Project Grudge had hired a consulting astronomer, Dr. J. Allen Hynek, whose job was to aid in identifying the planets, stars, meteors, and other astronomical or meteorological events that were mistaken for UFOs. Ruppelt called in more scientific experts and contracted with the Battelle Memorial Institute, a private research firm in nearby Columbus, Ohio, to help categorize and evaluate the data. He tried to set up ground recording systems and air-intercept scrambles at "hot spots"—areas that appeared to attract more than the average number of UFOs—but this was beyond his project's priority level and nothing came of several attempts.

After discovering that Ruppelt could not handle press relations and do his job at the same time, the Pentagon assigned him a liaison officer and an information officer. The first people who held those jobs were sympathetic to Ruppelt, his methods, and his goals. Minor administrative setbacks notwithstanding, Ruppelt thought that Project Blue Book was functioning well by the end of 1951. It was collecting data from all available sources, evaluating that data through the work of its own staff and the technical expertise available at ATIC, and, in Ruppelt's own words, "sifting through the reams of data in search of the answers . . . required many hours of overtime work, but when a report came out with the final conclusion, 'Unknown,' we were sure that it was unknown."[16]

1952: Washington, DC

UFO reports had peaked in July every year since systematic record-keeping had begun in 1947, and the year 1952 was a UFO turning point for the public and the government. The midsummer peak in 1952 broke all previous records. By June the number of cases had already attracted attention in the Pentagon, and Ruppelt was called to Washington to brief a high-level intelligence meeting. He was criticized by some of those present for being too cautious in defining Unknowns, and Ruppelt reports that there was support among some people at the meeting for accepting the ETH, stopping all public comment, turning Blue Book into a Top Secret project, and starting a serious effort to determine the operating characteristics and origin of the UFOs. But the intelligence general in charge of the meeting restrained the enthusiasts and told Ruppelt that Blue Book was doing just fine as it was, while agreeing that the project should deploy ground-based photographic resources in order to get what every expert that Blue Book had consulted thought would be the most useful data: spectroscopic and position triangulation data on one UFO. Before the photographic project could get started (it never did), the meeting's decisions were overtaken by the Washington flap.

On July 1 the Air Force's Ground Observer Corps spotted two UFOs moving southwest above Boston, and jet fighters were sent up to intercept. A couple near Lynn, Massachusetts and, independently, an Air Force captain leaving home for work, saw the jets, looked up to see what they were chasing, and saw the two UFOs much higher than the jets, whose pilots reported that they could not spot the UFOs either by sight or on radar.

A few hours later, three instructors and twelve students in a radar class at Fort Monmouth, New Jersey, which is about 200 miles southwest of Boston, plotted two UFOs arriving from the northeast. The UFOs flew high but slowly, then loitered at about 50,000 feet before moving off to the southwest. Some of the students and one instructor went outside when the UFOs showed up on the radar and confirmed the radar plots by visual observation.

UFOs, ETs, and Alien Abductions

A few hours later, a crowd of people in downtown Washington, DC was looking up at something hovering northwest of the city. A physics professor saw the crowd looking up at a "dull, gray, smoky-colored" object, and called the Air Force. The flap was on.

Reports from across the country came so fast in July that Blue Book officers and staff worked fourteen hours a day, six days a week to deal with the American sightings in addition to filing (but not analyzing) the many foreign reports reaching ATIC. Sightings were reported from the Hanford, Washington plutonium processing plant, from Chicago, and from Blue Book's home in Dayton, Ohio. Ruppelt wrote that the proportion of Unknowns in July was up to 40 percent, much higher than the usual 10 to 15 percent remaining after misperceptions of airplanes, meteors, stars, planets, and atmospheric phenomena had been eliminated. Local Air Force intelligence officers swamped Blue Book with calls. They were told to send in only their most promising reports because Blue Book couldn't keep up with the volume.

On the evening of Saturday, July 19, 1952, radars at Washington National Airport and nearby Andrews Air Force Base in Maryland tracked UFOs that flew slower than airplanes and then accelerated rapidly before coming back into radar and visual range. Airliner crews saw lights where the radars saw targets; jets were again scrambled to intercept, but as usual the interceptor pilots could not see, photograph, or shoot at anything.

Ruppelt had returned to Dayton after his June meeting, but the Pentagon called him back to Washington, and on the morning of Monday, July 21, he again got off an airliner at Washington National Airport. Ruppelt picked up a newspaper and read press accounts saying that the Air Force "wouldn't talk" about the Saturday sightings. No one had told the Air Force's UFO officer—Ruppelt—about them.

There were Pentagon meetings that Monday morning and afternoon to decide what to do and say about the sightings. Ruppelt did not want to commit himself before investigating, so at about 4:00 p.m. that day the Air Force issued an official "no comment." The generals running the meetings assumed that Ruppelt would stay on through Tuesday, visit the control towers, talk to the radar men, and write a report afterward.

Then began a classic snafu caused by the fact that Ruppelt was only a captain and the Air Force was only a bureaucracy. From 4:00 to 5:00 on Monday evening, Ruppelt tried to get a staff car from the Pentagon so he could make his control tower and radar center visits. Impossible: Pentagon staff cars were available only to colonels and above. He then tried to get Personnel to let him charge taxi fare as an expense. Impossible: he was told to take the bus. When he said his stops were miles apart and he didn't know the bus system, he was told he could charge taxi fares to his nine-dollar-a-day per diem, which also included his hotel and meals. He was also told that according to his travel document he should be on his way back to Dayton that night, and if he didn't get the document amended or return to Dayton he would be technically AWOL. At this point Ruppelt wrote "If saucers were buzzing Pennsylvania Avenue in formation I couldn't care less."[17] So the captain in charge of the Air Force's UFO investigation, who had spent the day at the Pentagon briefing colonels and generals about the unprecedented Washington, DC sightings, caught the next flight back to Dayton.

The Washington flap continued, and reports flooded in from across the country. Ruppelt returned to Washington the following week. While in Washington for the second time in July, Ruppelt got a call from President Truman's Air Force aide who asked him to explain what was happening. Ruppelt said he didn't know, but he couldn't completely rule out "temperature inversions," an atmospheric condition that sometimes bends radar waves sent skyward back to the ground so they reflect off moving cars and into the radar receiver, making the radar appear to be tracking moving targets in the sky when it is really tracking moving cars on the ground. Ruppelt knew that the radar experts who were on the scene during the Washington sightings had rejected that explanation, but he wanted to be cautious when passing information to the chief executive.

The Air Force held a press conference about the Washington

UFOs, ETs, and Alien Abductions

sightings at the end of July. The general in charge repeated Ruppelt's position that temperature inversions might have caused the sightings, and he was not questioned critically about the explanation. He said the Air Force was continuing its investigations, but the sightings did not constitute a threat to national security. After a month of press excitement, the Air Force explanation was taken at face value by most but not all of the press present, and national newspaper accounts reflected fatigue with the UFO story. The Pentagon's instructions to Blue Book were to carry on as before.

The CIA's Robertson Panel

President Truman wasn't satisfied with Ruppelt's answer, and at the president's direction CIA officials organized a scientific task force to deal with UFOs. There was competition between the CIA officials who were not completely skeptical about UFOs and those who were. The search for experts vacillated between choosing scientists who had expressed a serious interest in the phenomenon, meaning that they had some background knowledge and had at least considered the ETH, or choosing scientists who had no interest in UFOs and no background knowledge. The final panel, assembled in January 1953, consisted of five people who had no interest in UFOs and no background knowledge.

Howard P. Robertson, PhD, a physicist and CIA employee, was the panel chair. Other members were Samuel Goudsmit, Luis Alvarez, Thornton Page and Lloyd Berkner, all of whom had worked closely with the US government during World War II. The panel met on a Wednesday to review documents and UFO film footage. It heard from Blue Book astronomical consultant J. Allen Hynek. It heard from Edward J. Ruppelt. It heard from photo interpretation specialists about some UFO films, and it heard from Air Force officers about the difficulties of tracking and recording UFO sightings. By Saturday Robertson was preparing a draft of the panel report, and it was completed that weekend. The panel had a report ready by the following Monday.

Imagine yourself a high-level scientific adviser to the US government during the 1950s. You've earned a scientific or engineering doctorate from Caltech or MIT in the 1930s; you've done government-sponsored research and development work during World War II, perhaps on the atomic bomb, radar, proximity fuses for artillery shells, or computer development. For about ten years of your professional life you've worked to win the war and secure the peace. You and the small group of similarly accomplished colleagues whom you trust are better informed about modern science and technology than any comparable group of people in the world. You talk regularly with high-ranking military officers and government officials in the defense, intelligence, and political communities whose job it is to keep America safe.

As the 1950s begin, the Soviet Union has the atomic bomb, Communist subversives are trying to overthrow democratic governments in Europe, and accusations about Communist spies in the American government are at their peak. NATO has just been founded, the Korean War is ongoing, and the United States has embarked on a massive rearmament program. And in the middle of these serious national problems, a captain and a few enlisted men at the Air Technical Intelligence Center at Wright-Patterson Air Force Base claim that they have reliable reports of unknown aerial vehicles of superior performance sighted and tracked on radar across the United States. There are a few films purporting to show these objects in flight. You, a trusted scientific expert, are asked to advise the CIA about how to deal with this problem. You have no detailed knowledge of the Blue Book reports. Your cultural awareness includes newspaper reports of "flying saucers" and "contactees," and perhaps the Washington, DC flap that precipitated your assignment. Your sole technical briefing was a short trip to Wright-Patterson to meet the Blue Book staff and a few talks in Washington given by the same people. You view the films. Your other scientific and technical knowledge—and it is completely up-to-date—includes no theory that explains the performance of the objects described in the reports prepared by this small group of low-ranking personnel.

In early 1953 the air defense of the United States depends on regional "filter centers" that monitor radar station tracks and the visual observation reports received from the volunteer-based Ground Observer Corps. If a filter center identifies an unknown target, jets are sent to intercept it. In the summer of 1952 filter center operators spent hours each day analyzing UFO reports, leaving the centers vulnerable to the risk of ignoring radar tracks or ground observer reports that might signal approaching Soviet bombers. So even if UFOs were not a threat to national security, as the Air Force claimed, UFO *reports* were arguably a threat to national security. You have just been appointed to a panel assembled by the CIA in early 1953 and you are asked to decide how to respond to the UFO problem. What would you do?

The Panel report rejected the possibility that some UFOs might be extraterrestrial spacecraft. They decided that non-extraterrestrial explanations could be found for most of the sightings that they briefly reviewed, and that with a little more data and the proper application of the scientific method similar explanations could be found for the rest. The panel decided there was no single explanation for every sighting, and it would be a waste of time and money to try to find an explanation for every one. In fact, historical accounts of the Robertson Panel show that the panel members had rejected the ETH even before they sat down together.[18]

The panel wrote that the UFO phenomenon as such was *not* a threat to national security, but that UFO reports *were,* because Soviet bombers approaching the United States might be mistaken for UFOs, delaying timely warning to fighter planes and antiaircraft guns. The mystery surrounding UFO reports added to filter center overload and the possibility of mass hysteria that might threaten the stability of the US government. It recommended that Project Blue Book concentrate on reducing filter center overload and the potential for mass hysteria by publicly solving new Unknowns in order to make the public think that there was no reason to report similar sightings in the future. It recommended that unidentified cases be classified and withheld from the public. It recommended a public education campaign be launched to debunk the UFO mystery. It recommended that private UFO investigation groups be watched because they might become a threat to political stability. The CIA then gave Ruppelt a sanitized version of the report, which made him think that Blue Book had a mandate to carry on as before. This hardly mattered, though, because Ruppelt left the Air Force before the end of the year, and from then on Blue Book was an empty shell that pretended to seriously investigate UFOs but did little of value through its final wind-up in 1970.

2

A Chronology of Doubt

T he Ground Observer Corps and the radar operators and pilots who tracked and chased UFOs were professionally trained observers who produced trustworthy reports for Blue Book, making it possible for Ruppelt and his staff to accurately classify cases as Identified or Unknown. After the Robertson Panel decided that Blue Book field data and reports on unidentified cases should be classified, none of this material was available to the public. Since UFOs continued to be seen by civilians and reported in newspapers, magazines, and books, and on radio and television, the public debate was carried on by people who had no access to government data and who, unlike the Air Force, were not equipped to gather reliable UFO information. Public discussion without reliable data increased the uncertainty during the "chronology of doubt."

Media reporters have never applied Ruppelt's rigorous Blue Book standards to the analysis of UFO reports. A newspaper, TV, or YouTube record of a UFO is only one part of a puzzle with many missing pieces, and the evidence is seldom clear enough to enable the media bystander to accurately label the case as Identified or Unknown.

The Protagonists

The twentieth-century UFO debate was dominated by a few important personalities and organizations whose interactions were responsible for most of the significant events during the chronology of
doubt.

J. Allen Hynek

J. Allen Hynek was the astronomer hired by the Air Force in 1948 to
explain how astronomical and meteorological phenomena could be
mistaken for UFOs. His job was to turn UFOs into IFOs—identified
flying objects—for Air Force Projects Sign, Grudge, and Blue Book.
He kept that job until Blue Book closed in 1970. During his twenty-
two-year UFO apprenticeship, Hynek came to realize that not every
UFO was a misperceived man-made or natural phenomenon, and his
position evolved from skepticism to cautious acceptance of the ETH.
He wrote the definitive book on the subject as it stood at the time,
The UFO Experience: A Scientific Inquiry, in 1972.

I met Hynek twice. Once we discussed the Lake Baskatong case
mentioned in the introduction. Another time I was on standby at
a local radio station in case he was late for a talk show appearance,
which he wasn't. When I met him he was at the absolute center of
the scientific controversy over UFOs. He was polite, reserved, non-
committal, and cautiously interested in local cases with good supporting evidence.

Hynek was still on call as a consultant during Blue Book's
decline. He was not often consulted, and when he was, his advice was
often not followed. But he still had access to case files and he found
evidence in those files that bore no relation to the Blue Book reports
that "explained" that evidence.

For example, in 1966, three Ohio sheriff's deputies saw at close
range and then chased a UFO for more than seventy miles as it flew
east at low altitude to the Pennsylvania border. A Pennsylvania officer also saw the UFO. The officers' reports were consistent and were

consistent with the radio logs of the chase. The officers reported that they also saw both the moon and Venus *along with* the low-flying UFO. Hynek checked satellite logs and there were no satellites in view at the time the officers encountered the UFO. The weather was normal. Blue Book did not consult Hynek and called it an "astronomical" IFO.

Donald E. Keyhoe

While Edward J. Ruppelt was still in charge of Project Blue Book and sympathetic UFO liaison and public relations officers were still on the Pentagon payroll, and before the Pentagon intelligence community had been muzzled by the Robertson Panel, UFO case material available to the military was occasionally given to journalists and writers who either asked for it or, in some cases, were invited to look at it. Donald E. Keyhoe was one of them.

Keyhoe, a retired Marine Corps officer, former pilot and science fiction writer, was a Naval Academy graduate who became a Marine Corps pilot long before World War II. He resigned from the prewar Corps following an injury suffered in an airplane accident. He then became a writer and an aviation publicist, organizing, among other things, a tour for Charles Lindbergh. Keyhoe reenlisted at the beginning of World War II and served in a training capacity, retiring after the war as a Major. Keyhoe had good friends among post-war Navy brass. Initially skeptical about UFOs, he was asked to write an article on the UFO phenomenon for *True* magazine. Through his contacts in the Navy, with other military airmen, and the UFO staff at the Pentagon, he obtained many military-quality UFO accounts—much of it Blue Book material. On the basis of his research, he concluded that UFOs were extraterrestrial, and his article, "Flying Saucers Are Real," appeared in the January 1950 issue. He wrote about these cases, acknowledging the Pentagon's help, in his 1953 book, *Flying Saucers from Outer Space.*

Donald H. Menzel

Donald H. Menzel, PhD, a Harvard astronomer, was a member of the scientific and government elite that managed the nation's security during and after World War II. He wrote textbooks and published research articles in scientific journals, so he had more scientific standing than Keyhoe. Although Menzel was not a member of the Robertson Panel, he was either in direct contact with or knew a mutual acquaintance of every one of the panel members. His book, *Flying Saucers,* was published by Harvard University Press in 1953, the same year as Keyhoe's book.

Flying Saucers fulfilled the debunking agenda of the Robertson Panel. Menzel wrote with innocent wonder about what people have been seeing in the sky for centuries. He wrote that while we don't always know exactly what we've seen, the physics of ice crystals, clouds, halos and the physiological optics of the human eye and visual system, along with the foibles of human psychology, explain most of it. Menzel wrote that he could explain all but a tiny fraction of the things that people had seen in years past and that they were currently seeing during the "saucer scare." If he couldn't completely explain a particular UFO case right now the reason was only because he didn't have quite enough information about the case or he didn't understand the atmosphere quite well enough. The book covered a wide range of topics, from a discussion of nineteenth-century newspaper accounts of airships, to the famous 1938 "War of the Worlds" radio broadcast by Orson Welles that fooled some people into thinking that Earth was being invaded from Mars, to profiles of current contactees and their cult followers.

Menzel described a "flying saucer" that he saw and then told the reader what it was not: "I do *not* believe that what I saw, or anything anyone else has reported seeing, were missiles or messengers or vehicles from Venus, the moon, or Mars, or space." Ruppelt's Blue Book standard for evidence was: "When a report came out with the final conclusion, 'Unknown,' we were sure that it was unknown."[19] Menzel labeled sightings as "known" but his identifications did not depend on any consistent or credible standard of evidence. Menzel, the scientist, did not write a scientific book.

UFO Groups

Dissatisfied with the government's official response to UFOs, ordinary people started private UFO study groups that have defined the nongovernmental image of the UFO phenomenon ever since the 1950s. APRO, NICAP, MUFON, CUFOS, FUFOR and smaller groups started in the years 1947 to 1980, during the chronology of doubt (see figure 6a on page 12).

The Aerial Phenomena Research Organization (APRO)

The Aerial Phenomena Research Organization (APRO) was founded in 1952 by Coral Lorenzen, who had seen two UFOs; one as a child and another just before the Kenneth Arnold sighting in 1947. She ran the organization with her husband Jim Lorenzen, an electronics technician who was employed by various military and government agencies. APRO published a newsletter to publicize UFO sightings in response to the Air Force's Project Grudge reports that debunked them, and APRO did not dismiss reports of contacts with extraterrestrials. The organization was founded in Wisconsin but later moved, along with the Lorenzens, to California, New Mexico, and Arizona, and it lasted until Coral, the surviving Lorenzen, died in 1988.[20]

The National Investigations Committee on Aerial Phenomena (NICAP)

The National Investigations Committee on Aerial Phenomena (NICAP) was founded in 1956. Donald Keyhoe was on the founding board of directors and became its executive director shortly thereafter. He directed NICAP through most of its useful years, until 1969, although the organization continued under other directors until it was finally dissolved in 1980. I joined NICAP in 1966 and was invited to participate in a group of fifteen scientists who evaluated six so-called "occupant" cases—close encounters with humanoids in or near UFOs that had been documented by NICAP (more about that in chapter 4).

NICAP received reports volunteered by retired military personnel, pilots, and the like, and many of them were recorded in NICAP's *The UFO Evidence,*[21] a compendium of cases published in 1964. One of Keyhoe's oldest friends in the military, Rear Admiral Delmer S. Fahrney (Ret.), had been head of the Navy's guided missile development program. He provided a report that appeared in *The UFO Evidence* about a giant illuminated disc that approached a US Navy Super Constellation (R7V-2) aircraft flying from Europe to a North American touchdown at Gander, Newfoundland in 1956. The disc was seen at night ahead and below the aircraft; then it shot up on a collision course toward the super constellation, veered away at the last minute, and then held formation briefly with the aircraft at a distance estimated to be about 300 feet. The disc appeared to be between 400 and 500 feet in diameter and about 30 feet thick at the center. It was seen by the crew and passengers, and both the aircraft and the UFO alongside it were tracked on the Gander radar.

The Fund for UFO Research (FUFOR)

Members of NICAP who wanted to encourage UFO research founded the Fund for UFO Research (FUFOR) in 1979. Based in Silver Spring, Maryland, FUFOR cooperates with the other major UFO organizations to evaluate and fund UFO-related research projects.

The Mutual UFO Network (MUFON)

The Midwest UFO Network (MUFON) was founded in Illinois in 1969. It soon expanded nationwide and renamed itself the Mutual UFO Network. In 2013 it was active and based in Colorado. MUFON follows up UFO sighting reports using a nationwide network of trained volunteer investigators. The reports are catalogued, and interesting cases, along with other editorial features, are published in the monthly *MUFON Journal*. MUFON holds an annual convention with invited experts as speakers.

The Center for UFO Studies (CUFOS)

In 1973 J. Allen Hynek founded the Chicago-based Center for UFO Studies (CUFOS). CUFOS carries out careful scientific evaluations of UFO reports, maintains a library and archive of UFO reports, and issues reports on particular aspects of the UFO phenomenon.

UFO Waves and the Government's Response

Figure 6b (see page 13) plots the number of UFO reports per year from 1947 to 1981. The reports are from UFOCAT, a database first assembled by the Condon Committee (see pages 44–50). It includes reports from Blue Book and many other sources. There are peaks in reporting for the years 1952, 1954, 1957, 1967, and 1973, years of so-called "UFO waves" in the United States and abroad.

Because we don't know how often people who see UFOs actually report them to the police or the Air Force, we cannot tell whether the report "waves" are caused by feedback from widely publicized cases or whether the waves really depend on how often UFOs actually show up. Reports that reached Project Blue Book through Air Force channels up to 1969 have about the same frequency peaks as the other UFOCAT reports. Air Force observers are most often pilots, air traffic controllers, and radar operators, and are better-trained and better-motivated observers than the general public. This suggests that the waves may actually depend on how often UFOs appear.

The waves are accompanied by increased media publicity, and increased media publicity encourages people to write to their congressmen, so UFO waves coincided with periods of greater congressional interest in UFOs. The Air Force debunking policy led to skirmishes between Congress, whose constituents continued to see UFOs, and the Air Force, which continued to dismiss them. The Air Force had no desire to publicly explain what it was doing about UFOs to congressional committees while congressmen, listening to complaints by voters who were upset about their UFO reports getting an official brush-off, wanted the Air Force to tell their constituents a more convincing story. The skirmishing lasted fourteen years, and waxed and waned along with the report waves. The Air Force occasionally conceded a closed-doors briefing to one congressional committee or another but avoided having to talk to Congress in public until 1966—and that discussion led to the formation of the Condon Committee (see pages 44–50).

Project Blue Book Special Report No. 14

Project Blue Book Director Edward J. Ruppelt hired the Battelle Memorial Institute, a private scientific research firm in Columbus, Ohio, to analyze 2,199 case reports from 1947 through 1952. The result was Project Blue Book Special Report No. 14, completed in 1955—well after the Robertson Panel had decided that the government's role was to debunk UFOs, and well after Blue Book, without Ruppelt's leadership, had become a shell of its former self. Special Report No. 14 was circulated officially in small numbers until congressmen began to ask for it. Private citizens finally obtained the report and made more copies.[22]

As someone whose technical higher education began during the transition from punch-card readers to vacuum-tube computers, I understand from personal experience the limitations of the punch-card sorting methods used by the Battelle engineers who analyzed the Blue Book data. First, a Battelle staff member read a Blue Book report and tried to classify it using a list of standard categories: Aircraft, Balloon, Birds, Insufficient Information, Psychological, Unknown, Other. They then made a preliminary judgment about the reliability of the observer. Any observation that a first reader called Unknown was reviewed by two more ATIC staff members and two Battelle consultants. The four additional reviewers had to agree before a case was classified as Unknown. Disagreements were set aside and referred back to Battelle team members later. Each

UFOs, ETs, and Alien Abductions

observation (or case; sometimes a single case had more than one observation) was then coded onto punch cards as either a Known or as one of a class of Unknowns. The cards contained data about other aspects of the observation as well, like witness reliability, duration, elevation angle, azimuth angle, apparent speed, color, brightness, shape, number of objects, and sighting time of day. The Battelle engineers then used their punch-card sorting machines to compare the distribution of Knowns versus Unknowns on each of the sighting characteristics, after which they evaluated the differences between Knowns and Unknowns on each of the characteristics.

Special Report No. 14's conclusions were at odds with its data. Of the 2,199 cases, about 20 percent had enough data so that the quality of the evidence and the reliability of the witness classified the reported object as an Unknown. The more reliable the witness or witnesses, the higher the probability the report was an Unknown. The Unknowns differed from the Knowns on:

• Color—more Unknowns were blue

• Number—there were more multiple sightings of Unknowns

• Shape—Unknowns looked like rockets or aircraft—but they weren't because they were Unknowns

• Duration of observations—Unknowns were seen for longer

• Speed—Unknowns were faster

Unknowns were distinctively different from the Knowns in many ways, but there was so much diversity among the Unknowns that the Battelle engineers could not develop a single model to fit all of them.

The Battelle engineers then removed all of the astronomical observations from the known data and redid their calculations. They found that the non-astronomical Knowns differed from the Unknowns on number (there were more Unknowns than Knowns in each case) and on speed (the Unknowns went faster than the Knowns), but the

Unknowns and Knowns were now more alike on color, shape, and duration. The engineers argued that since there were now fewer differences between the Knowns and the Unknowns, *the remaining differences must be unimportant.*

They stopped asking "What are the Unknowns?" and asked instead "Why can't we explain the Unknowns?" This last question is not as upsetting as worrying about what the Unknowns might be. The Battelle engineers concluded that the Unknowns, however reliably and frequently they had been observed, were just misidentified Knowns. The Air Force used the Battelle Institute report to justify its assertion that UFOs were not a defense threat. This information, provided in closed-door briefings to various congressmen and congressional committees, helped to short-circuit public hearings that the Pentagon wanted to avoid.

Neither the Robertson Panel in 1953 nor the Battelle engineers in 1955 were willing to accept reliable anomalous data in its own right. The Robertson Panel, none of whose members were familiar with the UFO phenomenon before sitting down to evaluate it, produced *ad hoc* conventional explanations to replace the expert analysis of Unknowns with which they had been provided, and they focused only on the threat that UFO observations posed to the air defense system. The Battelle engineers could not construct one model to fit all of the Unknowns, so they deprecated the importance of all of the Unknowns. The constraint imposed by motivated, habitual thinking explains how the UFO evidence was treated by institutional decision-makers starting in 1947, and how institutional decision-makers continue to treat it today.

What Is the Problem: The Evidence or the Explanation?

An "explanation" for the UFO phenomenon is the obstacle over which many UFO investigations and many UFO investigators have stumbled. The scientifically trained investigators of 1952 (the Robertson Panel), 1955 (the Battelle Report), and 1968 (the

Condon Committee Report, soon to be discussed) had an easy out for unexplained UFO reports: they were a "residue" that for some *unexplained reason* did not match the many and far more probable *conventional explanations* that accounted for perhaps 80 to 85 percent of all observations. Based largely on the public advocacy of Donald Menzel, the conventional explanation dominated the scientific discussion of UFOs. If a scientist had to have something left over or unexplained from a sighting, that did not necessarily mean the unexplained sighting was extraterrestrial; it only meant the unexplained sighting could not be easily fitted into a conventional explanation. So the scientific shrug of the shoulders was about why the data did not fit a conventional explanation—not why the unexplained data existed at all.

Despite the skeptical tone of Blue Book Special Report No. 14, sightings of Unknowns continued to be reported after it was released. NICAP reports that in 1955 airline crews and control tower observers watched as the Jacksonville, Florida Naval Air Station directed two jets toward a fast-maneuvering, round, orange-red object, which quickly climbed to 30,000 feet and then circled and buzzed the jets. The jets were outmaneuvered by the object, but the encounter was tracked on radar, spotted visually, and seen from the cockpits of the Navy jets.

In 1957 (the same year as the RB-47 encounter described in chapter 1), there was a widely publicized series of sightings in Levelland, Texas. A dozen local residents, including police officers, saw and reported glowing, egg-shaped objects on and near roads around the town over a period of a few hours on the evening of November 2. The local Air Force investigator wrote that he had "no idea of the possible cause of the sighting," but Blue Book worsened its public image by carrying out a late and cursory investigation and then explaining the sightings as ball lightning. This case generated a great deal of bad publicity for the Air Force, and shortly thereafter congressional pressure forced the Air Force to offer the House subcommittee on Atmospheric Phenomena a closed-door briefing on the history of the Air Force's UFO involvement.

This pattern of chronic UFO sightings and Blue Book "explanations" that explained little of what was reported continued from 1953 until the Air Force stopped investigating UFOs in 1970. During this time the Air Force fought the UFO phenomenon with one hand tied behind its back: its 1953 policy, mandated by the Robertson Panel, prevented Blue Book from even mentioning unexplained cases. The media was not hindered by this policy and, aided by NICAP and other private groups, reported many clearly unexplained sightings like the Levelland case. Rather than not comment at all when the data was clearly unconventional, Blue Book published lame conventional explanations at obvious variance with the widely publicized facts, leading many people to consider Blue Book investigations as farcical—and with good reason.

J. Allen Hynek, the Air Force's hired astronomical expert on alternative explanations for UFO sightings, worked with increasing awareness that there was a large inventory of reports he could not explain. Although Hynek did not make a clean break with Air Force policy on UFOs until after Blue Book closed in 1970, he spoke to a research group at Elgin Air Force Base in 1960 about the many reports that could not be explained by conventional astronomical or meteorological means.[23] He described how while he was in France he had taken the trouble to contact UFO researcher Aimé Michel. Michel had collected and reported on a consistent series of French close-encounter sightings in 1954. Hynek was impressed by Michel's competence and by the consistency of his reports. Hynek saw that UFO cases were based largely on human testimony sometimes backed up by radar or other confirmatory evidence, but ultimately dependent on the truthfulness and accuracy of the eyewitnesses. The French reports gathered by Michel, as well as the Blue Book reports to which Hynek had access, were from trained professionals as well as ordinary people, and Hynek knew that the unexplained reports did not differ greatly, regardless of the professional status of the observer. In 1960 Hynek left the explanation of the Unknowns as a matter of conjecture.

The point of Hynek's talk at Elgin Air Force Base was to emphasize the consistency of the unexplained phenomena and to recommend a scientific approach, rather than the national security–oriented Air Force effort, to investigate it. Six years later, in 1966, he got his wish. But the results were not what he had expected.

NICAP's *The UFO Evidence*, published in 1964, contains a thirteen-page section outlining the disagreements between the Air Force and NICAP. There were stories about people whose films had been lost or tampered with by the Air Force, people who had been told not to talk about what they had seen, and people who had been misled about UFOs by the Air Force in other ways. The rest of the NICAP publication summarized the organization's opinion of what was the best evidence for the material existence of UFOs, whatever their origin, as of 1964. *The UFO Evidence* editorialized for a congressionally organized public hearing into the entire subject. NICAP, like Hynek, was soon to get its way.

The Socorro, New Mexico Case

On April 24, 1964—just a few weeks before *The UFO Evidence* was published—police officer Lonnie Zamora was chasing a speeder in Socorro, New Mexico, at 4:15 in the afternoon. Officer Zamora was distracted from his chase because he "heard a roar and saw a flame in the sky to the southwest some distance away."[24] Zamora knew there was a shack containing dynamite in that direction, so he abandoned his chase and went to investigate. As he drove closer he saw something he described as a large egg supported by slender legs sitting just off the ground. He saw two small creatures dressed in white coveralls standing near it. They appeared to be startled as his car approached. A hill blocked his view momentarily, and when he saw the object again the creatures were not visible. He stopped his car and got out, intending to approach on foot, but the object emitted a roar and blue and orange flames pulsed from the bottom. Zamora ducked behind his patrol car. The roaring stopped, and when Zamora looked again the object was airborne, hovering a few feet off the ground. It gathered speed and headed toward the dynamite shack, which it barely cleared. Another officer pulled up and watched with Zamora as the object flew off into the distance. A third witness who saw the object in the air was located later. The two officers went to the spot where the egg had been parked and found charred and singed grass and impressions in the ground from its legs.[25]

The officer in charge of Blue Book at the time, Major Hector Quintanilla, checked with aerospace companies, NASA, and other government agencies to learn whether they had anything like an experimental lunar lander operating in the vicinity; the answer was no. There were also no helicopter flights, aircraft, or balloons in the area at the time. Then Quintanilla sent Hynek to investigate.

The case for calling the Socorro sighting an Unknown was strong: There were multiple independent witnesses, two of whom were police officers. One of Hynek's scientific associates happened to know Zamora and gave the officer an outstanding character reference. There were physical traces. And there was the report of humanoids associated with the object. Hynek called it an extremely strong case and Blue Book decided to call it an Unknown (but confidentially, following established policy). According to UFO researcher and scholar David Jacobs, "This is the only combination landing, trace and occupant case listed as unidentified in Blue Book files."[26] Lonnie Zamora had a good reputation, lived an ordinary life, and wanted it to continue that way, and he was reluctant to talk about the sighting. But the clarity of his observation and the reliability of his character gave him an important place in the history of UFOs.

The Michigan Sightings

Two years after the Socorro, New Mexico case, Hynek himself precipitated the terminal public relations disaster for Blue Book. Residents of Dexter, Michigan, had reported seeing lights emanating from a swampy area on a nearby farm, and students at a local girls' college in Hillsdale, Michigan, about sixty miles from Dexter, also said they had seen lights in the woods. Quintanilla and Hynek went to investigate. After visiting both sites, Hynek said at a Detroit news conference that the supposed low-flying UFOs might have been caused by "swamp gas." Methane generated by decaying vegetable matter sometimes spontaneously ignites to produce mysterious lights in the woods. But that was the wrong thing to say to the wrong people at the wrong time, because no one believed it, and everyone, including the media, was fed up with dismissive Blue Book explanations. The case generated nationwide derisive comment about the Air Force's efforts to explain UFO sightings.

Michigan citizens, given the brush-off by the Air Force, were incensed.[27,28] A Michigan Democratic congressman and the Republican House minority leader (and future president) Gerald Ford asked the House Armed Services Committee to hold a public hearing on UFOs, which they did, in April, 1966. After years of trying to avoid congressional exposure the Air Force now had to appear publicly before its legislative overseers to explain what it was doing about UFOs.

The secretary of the Air Force appeared, as did Blue Book chief Hector Quintanilla and J. Allen Hynek. While little of note was said, something of great importance was done. For the Air Force, UFO investigations were a financial liability and a public relations disaster. An internal Air Force committee had already recommended that the entire problem be handed over to university scientists. The secretary of the Air Force mentioned this idea to the congressional committee. The idea became a *fait accompli* because the congressional committee wanted a scientific review and the Air Force wanted to get rid of the UFO problem. Out of the Michigan sightings, Hynek's "swamp gas" remark, and the nationwide publicity it produced, the Condon Committee was born.

The Condon Committee: 1966–1968

Many scientific organizations were asked to carry out this next UFO study. Harvard, MIT, the University of North Carolina, the University of California, and the government-sponsored National Center for Atmospheric Research all refused. An Air Force representative contacted Edward U. Condon of the University of Colorado's Physics Department and asked him to chair the committee and to persuade his university to accept the project. Condon was cut from the same cloth as the scientists/engineers who had served on the CIA's Robertson Panel in 1952. He had worked on the Manhattan Project (the US atomic bomb) during the war, headed the National Bureau of Standards after the war, and had published many papers and books on quantum physics. His loyalty to the United States had been questioned during the McCarthy era, but his loyalty was in fact unquestionable and President Harry S. Truman had personally defended him. He was an ideal establishment candidate.

The Low Memorandum

Condon was reluctant to take on the project, and so was the University of Colorado. Robert J. Low, assistant dean of the university's graduate school, wrote a memo to his dean and to the university president describing how the university could get Air Force funding without being tarred by the UFO brush:

> Our study would be conducted almost exclusively by nonbelievers who, although they couldn't possibly prove a negative result, could and probably would add an impressive body of evidence that there is no reality to the observations. The trick would be, I think, to describe the project so that, to the public, it would appear a totally objective study but, to the scientific community, would present the image of a group of nonbelievers trying their best to be objective but having an almost zero expectation of finding a saucer. One way to do this would be to stress investigation, not of the physical phe-

nomena, but rather of the people who do the observing—the psychology and sociology of persons and groups who report seeing UFOs. If the emphasis were put here, rather than on examination of the old question of the physical reality of the saucer, I think the scientific community would quickly get the message.

. . . I'm inclined to feel at this early stage that, if we set up the thing right and take pains to get the proper people involved and have success in presenting the image we want to present to the scientific community, we could carry the job off to our benefit.[29]

T̶ mo was found by Condon Committee members who lic a year later, but not before Condon's own impartial- compromised by his frequent skeptical remarks. For said "My attitude right now is that there's nothing to n not supposed to reach a conclusion for another year," audience in Elmira, New York in late 1967. Although te the first chapter of the committee's eventual report, or nothing to do with its day-to-day operations, leaving that to be mismanaged by Robert Low.[30]

The paperback version of the Condon Committee Report, published in 1969, has 965 closely printed pages and contains about half a million words. Much of the report consists of appendices and fill-in chapters describing scientific apparatus and methods that do not apply directly to the cases studied. The important parts of the report are the first chapter, written by Condon, and the case studies that were prepared and written by members of the committee staff.

Condon's Conclusions

Excerpts from the first chapter of the report, titled "Conclusions and Recommendations," taken in order and in context, make it clear what Condon thought:

Careful consideration of the record as it is available to us leads us to conclude that further extensive study of UFOs probably cannot be justified in the expectation that science will be advanced thereby. . . . If they [scientists] agree with our conclusions, they will turn their valuable attention and talents elsewhere. . . . While we do not think at present that anything worthwhile is likely to come of such research each individual case ought to be carefully considered on its merits. . . . We find that there are important areas of atmospheric optics, including radio wave propagation, and of atmospheric electricity in which present knowledge is quite incomplete . . . they are also of fundamental scientific interest, and they are relevant to practical problems related to the improvement of safety of military and civilian flying.

We believe that the rigorous study of the beliefs—unsupported by valid evidence—held by individuals and even by some groups might prove of scientific value to the social and behavioral sciences . . .

The question remains of what, if anything, the federal government should do about the UFO reports it receives from the general public. We are inclined to think that nothing should be done with them . . . we know of no reason to question the finding of the Air Force that the whole class of UFO reports so far considered does not pose a defense problem. . . .

The subject of UFOs has been widely misrepresented to the public by a small number of individuals who have given sensationalized presentations in writings and public lectures . . . whatever effect there has been has been bad . . . we strongly recommend that teachers refrain from giving students credit for school work based on their reading of the presently available UFO books and magazine articles. Teachers who find their students strongly motivated in this direction should attempt to channel their interests in the direction of the serious study of astronomy and meteorology, and in the direction of critical analysis of arguments for fantastic propositions that are being supported by appeals to fallacious reasoning or false data.[31]

Condon dismissed the scientific value of UFO reports and discouraged scientists from studying them; he implied that the UFO phenomenon concerned only atmospheric physics, meteorology, and psychology; he castigated irresponsible people for misrepresenting the evidence, and opined that reading UFO books and magazines was bad for children and warned teachers to discourage them from doing it. He unburdened the Air Force, which had already told him exactly what it wanted, from the responsibility of studying UFOs.

The Case Studies

The report included fifty-nine case studies: ten that preceded the committee but were reviewed by it, thirty-five that were studied by the committee between 1966 and 1968, and fourteen photographic cases of varying ages. Of these fifty-nine cases, thirteen, or 22 percent, were described as Unidentified by the committee analysts—about the same percent of Unknowns as in the 1955 Battelle report. The committee's photographic expert, optical physicist William K. Hartmann, said of a well-known 1950 photographic case from McMinnville, Oregon:

> This is one of the few UFO reports in which all factors investigated, geometric, psychological and physical appear to be consistent with the assertion that an extraordinary flying object, silvery, metallic, disk-shaped, tens of meters in diameter, and evidently artificial, flew within sight of two witnesses. It cannot be said that the evidence positively rules out a fabrication, although there are some physical factors

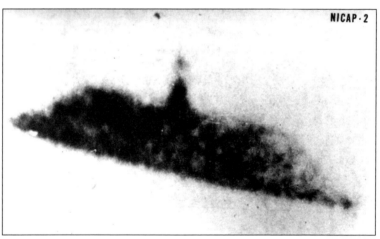

Figure 7. Top: UFO photographed from a fighter jet over Rouen, France in 1957; bottom: UFO photographed by Paul Trent in McMinnville, Oregon in 1950.

such as the accuracy of certain photometric measures of the original negatives which argue against a fabrication.

From the Robertson Panel in 1952, to the Battelle report of 1955, to the Condon Committee Report of 1968, nothing had changed. The gatekeepers of national defense did not move outside the limits of established science when dealing with UFOs, and the US government and the scientific establishment have not budged since.

The Congressional Hearing: 1968

There was public dissatisfaction with the perceived fairness of the Condon Committee. The dissatisfaction started with the release of the Low memorandum that revealed the "trick" required to bring the UFO investigation to the University of Colorado. Condon fired the two committee members who released the document and then the Committee's administrative assistant resigned in protest. The dissatisfaction was also based on Condon's own skeptical public comments and his inclusion of "contactees" as part of the investigation.

The dissatisfaction was heard in Congress. As a response to the general public as well as to the Condon Committee critics, including J. Allen Hynek, the House Committee on Science and Astronautics convened a one-day public hearing called the Symposium on Unidentified Flying Objects on July 29, 1968. The symposium heard testimony from five experts, including Hynek, who supported the idea that UFO reports were worth studying. They also heard from Carl Sagan, a well-known public figure in astronomy, who was skeptical that UFOs were extraterrestrial but told the committee that Congress should fund planetary and space exploration research in part to search for extraterrestrial intelligence. The symposium published all of this testimony as well as papers submitted by six more people, five of whom supported continued UFO research. The sixth paper was written by Donald Menzel. He was miffed that he was not asked to testify in person, but he submitted a summary of his earlier debunking arguments. The 247-page Congressional Symposium report was a narrowly circulated antidote to the longer, widely circulated Condon Committee Report issued a few months later.

The Air Force wound up Project Blue Book in January 1970.[32] From then to now the US government has had no publicly acknowledged interest in the UFO phenomenon. After publication of the Condon Committee Report, editorials by newspapers, influential columnists, and scientific journals have claimed that science has finally gotten rid of the UFO problem.

R. V. Jones: My Favorite Skeptic

An English scientist named R. V. Jones was a UFO skeptic during the chronology of doubt; he was a skeptic for whom I have the greatest respect. He wrote *Most Secret War,* an instructive and entertaining book about the Second World War, which I experienced safely and vicariously as the son of a Washington, DC–based US Naval Reserve officer. Jones was born in 1911, the same year as my father, but being English, he was involved in the war many years before. Jones was the son of a Grenadier Guards sergeant, and he wrote that "my childhood was steeped in the Regimental tradition of discipline, precision, service, endurance and good temper." Jones grew up in a rough London neighborhood but went to excellent grammar schools and then, encouraged by his mother, won a scholarship to a private school where he joined the Officer Training Corps. He liked science and entered the University of Oxford where he earned a physics doctorate under Frederick Lindemann, the eccentric scientist who was Winston Churchill's scientific adviser. Like Lindemann and Churchill, Jones saw that Hitler's Germany would go to war. As soon as he had earned his doctorate, Jones began research work on air defense projects. He was eventually put in charge of Air Scientific Intelligence, a branch of the British Secret Service, and he held that post throughout the war. *Most Secret War* describes Jones' contribution to intelligence discoveries and scientific countermeasures involving aircraft, radar, and rockets. It tells about his struggles as a young scientist fighting administrative battles with bureaucrats and with senior scientists who resisted his accurate but iconoclastic conclusions.

Jones knew two of the Robertson Panel scientists who advised the CIA about UFOs: Howard P. Robertson, the chairman, and Samuel Goudsmit. They met with Jones and other British scientists at the end of the war to evaluate Germany's progress toward an atomic bomb.

One chapter of Jones' book is titled "Swords into Plowshares, Bombs into Saucers." In 1946 a wave of Scandinavian UFO sightings preceded the American Kenneth Arnold sighting, and military intelligence officials went to Sweden, the main source of the reports, to try to learn what was happening. After six years of an exhausting war and the unrewarding bureaucratic work required to tidy up the end of it, the Swedish "ghost rockets" were just too much for Jones. He thought that the few reliable reports were caused by meteors and the rest were generated by the Allies' fear of German technology that might have been captured by the Soviets at the end of the war. Jones had spent the entire war sifting good intelligence from bad and was emotionally unprepared to deal with another round of what he thought was fantasy during the postwar letdown of 1945–1946.

Jones carried out elaborate practical jokes during his college days, and he used the same talent to help fool the Luftwaffe, both defensively and offensively, during the war. Some of Jones' postwar intelligence staff went out to investigate a report from an indignant farmer named Gunyon who asked the Royal Air Force to remove one of those "darned contraptions" that had landed on his field. The directions to the farm were not too clear; the officers looked up and down various rural byways, but they could not find farmer Gunyon's farm and could not locate the "contraption." Jones lets us know that he had turned his talents back on his own staff and that farmer Gunyon and the landed UFO were figments of his own imagination.

Jones wrote an appendix to the Condon Committee Report that contained some of the material in "Swords into Plowshares, Bombs into Saucers" and then added a reasoned discussion about the difficulty of proving a negative; that is, proving that the residue of unexplained UFO cases are *not* extraterrestrial vehicles. He made two important points. The first was to repeat the well-known philosophical principle, Occam's razor: when competing explanations are equal in other respects, the best explanation introduces the fewest assumptions.[33] Jones thought that the evidence was not good enough to require the ETH to explain Unknown UFO cases. American establishment gatekeepers had come to the same conclusion; namely, that it was easier to assume that the unexplained evidence was not the problem; rather, *why the evidence could not be explained* was the problem. Jones argued that it would be better to assume that there was a conventional explanation for the Unknowns than to assume that the Unknowns were extraterrestrial vehicles.

The second point Jones made was about how to collect reliable data. The British knew the Germans were developing a ballistic missile. Jones' efforts to learn how large a warhead the V-2 rocket would carry were complicated by some British scientists who thought the German rocket must be like a big firework, essentially just a pointed cardboard tube filled with gunpowder. The scientists did not know that the Germans could build a liquid-fueled rocket, but Jones did: he had received reports of the rocket's characteristics from Polish resistance fighters and from neutral Sweden, where an errant rocket had landed. In filtering new rocket information Jones decided to reject any report that did not refer to one of the rocket fuels being liquid air or liquid oxygen, which had been established with certainty. With that "touchstone," as Jones called it, in place, he was able to produce an accurate estimate of the weight of the entire rocket (about twelve tons) and of the warhead (one ton), which was different from the estimates made by other scientists not equipped with Jones' touchstone or his common sense.[34] The lesson Jones employed here was to evaluate novel intelligence reports on the basis of the report's consistency with facts already known, thereby confirming to some degree at least the reliability of the intelligence source.

In 1991 I wrote a letter to Jones because I was impressed by *Most Secret War*. I asked him whether his opinion about UFOs had changed in the meantime. Here is his answer:

> I have continued to have an interest in UFO's , and I summarized my views in a lecture that I gave in 1968, and of which I enclose a copy. Nothing that has happened since has changed my viewpoint, and the text of the lecture was published as an appendix to the substantial United States Air Force Report of 1969. I have read Dr. Hynek's comments, but I am sorry that he casts some doubt on the judgment of some of his American colleagues for whom I personally have great respect, having worked with them on rather similar projects towards the end of World War Two.
>
> I agree that we have to keep an open mind. There can certainly be some so far unidentified natural phenomenon which we have not so far understood, but I should be doubtful about an intelligent extraterrestrial origin until the evidence is very much stronger.

Jones found no touchstone for the extraterrestrial hypothesis, but now the UFO evidence is very much stronger, there are many touchstones, and the chronology of doubt about the ETH is long past.

3

Low, Big, and Slow:
The End of Doubt

I n September of 1965 the American journalist and writer John G. Fuller was trying to meet a deadline for a column he wrote regularly for the *Saturday Review* magazine. He spotted a *New York Times* clipping about UFO sightings in the Midwest and called NICAP, at that time the biggest and best-known UFO investigation group. Richard Hall, NICAP's administrator, suggested that Fuller cover some recent sightings in Exeter, New Hampshire. Fuller talked with Raymond Fowler, the NICAP investigation subcommittee chairman from nearby Massachusetts, and called local police stations to check out sighting records. Then he wrote a 1,000-word column about the Exeter sightings. He wrote it, as he said, very carefully, using quotes from a police officer who saw the UFOs as well as descriptions of sightings that ended up on the local police blotters. In his column Fuller mentioned that state police from across the country had been interviewing witnesses and documenting the sources of many recent close-range UFO sightings.

UFO sightings increased in 1965, reaching a new record high in 1967 (see figure 6b on page 13). Fuller's column generated letters from people who told him that what they had seen did not match Project Blue Book's after-the-fact dismissals. Fuller was persuaded to take a closer look at UFOs, and he decided to focus on the events in and around Exeter. He spent as much time as he could talking to local police and media and local Air Force base personnel and eyewitnesses—and in the process, he saw a UFO himself. *Incident at Exeter,* published in 1966, was the result.

Many of the reports in *Incident at Exeter* describe large objects seen at treetop height. A young man hitchhiking home to Exeter along a deserted road at about 2:00 a.m. watched a giant, egg-shaped, luminous thing with pulsating red lights around its circumference rise from behind the trees bordering a nearby field. It flew over him and away. He was terrified. He got a ride to Exeter and then ran into the police station to report what he saw. An officer drove him back to the site in a police car, and they explored the field and the bordering trees. At first they saw nothing, but as they returned to the car the object reappeared. The officer shouted "I see it!" into his open mike just as another officer pulled up in a second car. Both officers and the original witness watched the object fly off at treetop level toward the east. A few minutes later, a hysterical man called the police from a phone booth east of Exeter to report that a huge, low, luminous object had just flown over his car. Earlier that evening, a cruising officer had found a woman sitting terrified in her car by the side of the road. She described seeing the same thing, but the officer, assuming she was hallucinating, had ignored her report.

Fuller interviewed many witnesses who had seen UFOs in and around Exeter over the previous months. Curious people congregated in places where UFOs had been spotted, hoping to see one for themselves. Officers from nearby Pease Air Force Base, then home to B-47 and B-52 wings, made discreet inquires about UFO sightings in the local area. They committed nothing compromising to paper, but they were personally less dismissive about the evidence than were Blue Book officials. All of the local witnesses knew the difference between the B-47s and B-52s, which they saw and heard regularly, and the UFOs they had seen. Fuller visited one of the UFO observation spots. With other witnesses he watched a jet fighter, identified by its noise and its running lights, chase a UFO at an apparent altitude of 6–8,000 feet. Local witnesses reported many fighter-UFO chases over the previous few months.

Fuller, a good journalist, was a far better scientific observer and data collector than Edward U. Condon. Fuller's summary of the UFO phenomenon as he observed it in Exeter, New Hampshire, in the latter months of 1965 is compact, complete, and unambiguous:

- Dozens of intelligent, reliable people reported UFO sightings, many reluctantly because of the fear of ridicule.

- Most of the sightings were similar in description, and the police and military were reporting the same type of phenomenon as the ordinary layman.

- The reports of electromagnetic effects on lights, ignition, radios, and television indicated a similar conclusion.

- Photographs checked by experts, with full character investigation of the photographer, added further evidence.

- The verified cases of genuine shock and hysteria indicted further that low-level, near-landing reports were valid.

- Radar reports and scrambling jets chasing the objects indicated that the Air Force was not only cognizant of the objects but appeared to be impotent when it came to doing anything about them.

- The most logical but still unprovable explanation is that the unidentified flying objects are interplanetary spacecraft under intelligent control.

J. Allen Hynek Changes Sides

During his twenty years with the Air Force, and long before his "swamp gas" embarrassment of 1966, J. Allen Hynek recognized that a substantial residue of UFO cases offered enough evidence to eliminate all known causes. While employed by Project Blue Book, Hynek expressed his doubts only to technical audiences. But he knew that the pertinent question was not "Why can't we explain these?" but rather, "What are they?" Hynek's widely ridiculed "swamp gas" comment paved the way for his own public reversal. "Swamp gas" precipitated the congressional hearing that led to the Condon Committee, which led to the cancellation of Blue Book, which finally led to Hynek saying publicly what he really thought about UFOs.

Hynek started by writing a letter critical of the Condon Committee Report to *Science*, the leading American general science journal. *Science* first refused to publish it, but then relented and published a shorter and less critical version.[35] In 1972 Hynek published *The UFO Experience: A Scientific Inquiry*. The book laid out the evidence as Hynek knew it, and it introduced UFO terminology that is still in use today.

Hynek identified six classes of UFO reports:

- NL—nocturnal light sighting, the least revealing and most common report

- DD—daylight disk sighting, the visual report of a distant, disk-shaped object in the sky

- RV—radar-visual sighting, in which a radar return is correlated with a visual observation at the same time and place

- CE-I—a close encounter of the first kind: observation of an object at close range with visual detail; not just a light or a distant disk

- CE-II—a close encounter of the second kind: a visual encounter that leaves a trace, e.g., broken branches, disturbed soil or foliage, or a photographic record

- CE-III—a close encounter of the third kind: sighting humanoids or "occupants" associated with a close encounter (Steven Spielberg's 1977 movie, *Close Encounters of the Third Kind*, popularized this term.)

After Hynek died, his terminology was expanded to include CE-IV, a close encounter of the fourth kind, meaning abduction by occupants.

A more esoteric but equally useful contribution was Hynek's strangeness-probability diagram, which classifies each report on two characteristics: strangeness (how unusual is it?) and probability (how much do we trust the reporter[s]?) For instance, a nocturnal light reported by one myopic drunk would rate low (1,1) on both strangeness and probability; nocturnal lights aren't very strange, and shortsighted drunks aren't very reliable. On the other hand, if the secretary of the Air Force and two major generals reported a large disk with humanoids landing near the Pentagon on a clear day, their report would rate (9,9) on both strangeness and probability.[36]

The American Association for the Advancement of Science (AAAS) Symposium

In December 1969, about a year after the Condon Committee Report was released, the American Association for the Advancement of Science (AAAS) held a symposium on unidentified flying objects. Condon and UFO debunker Donald Menzel tried unsuccessfully to persuade the AAAS to cancel the event. Condon refused to participate, but Menzel showed up to oppose the "nuts" and "believers," his terms for scientists willing to consider the extraterrestrial hypothesis.

The symposium papers were edited by Carl Sagan and Thornton Page and published in 1972 as *UFOs: A Scientific Debate*. Skeptics tried to grapple with the observational evidence. William K. Hartmann, an astronomer and photo expert who had contributed to the Condon Committee Report, commented on the extreme difficulty of determining absolutely that a photograph is genuine.

Philip Morrison, an MIT physicist, commented on the difficulty of establishing an unequivocal chain of evidence about a novel event. Some contributors described UFO witnesses as inherently irrational, explaining that "primary-process thinking"—mental processes related to fundamental motivations—makes it difficult for witnesses to report their experiences objectively. Others suggested that UFOs could be integrated into a college curriculum to attract interest to basic science. Donald Menzel contributed "UFOs—The Modern Myth," which covered cases that he claimed had atmospheric or optical explanations. J. Allen Hynek summarized his twenty-one years of studying UFO reports and stressed the consistency and uniqueness of those that remained unexplained after thorough investigation.

The most controversial AAAS symposium paper was by James E. McDonald, titled "Science in Default: Twenty-Two Years of Inadequate UFO Investigations." McDonald, a University of Arizona astrophysicist, became interested in UFOs after seeing one in 1954. Thanks to his government-financed research on cloud physics, he was able to visit Project Blue Book headquarters at Wright-Patterson Air Force Base. While searching Project Blue Book files for information about atmospheric phenomena, McDonald found a copy of the unedited Robertson Panel report, which convinced him, correctly, that the Air Force was using Project Blue Book as a cover to divert public attention from the UFO problem.

From then on, McDonald lobbied Congress and his scientific colleagues to support UFO research. Inconveniently, McDonald's professional life depended on government grants and contracts, and Philip Klass, a senior editor of *Aviation Week* and a prominent debunker, urged McDonald's research sponsors to cancel his grants. When a congressional committee investigating supersonic transports called on McDonald for scientific testimony about the adverse effects of supersonic flight on the atmosphere, one congressman ridiculed McDonald's UFO interest to undermine his credibility. As McDonald's UFO commitment increased, his home life fell apart. His wife left him. A failed suicide attempt left him blind, and he finally did succeed in killing himself in 1971.

Science, the flagship general science journal of the AAAS, published little on UFOs from the 1947 Arnold sighting to the present. In 1966 they reluctantly published the shortened version of J. Allen Hynek's critique of the Condon Committee Report. In 1967 they published a paper explaining that UFOs could not be extraterrestrial because an explanation couldn't be found for how UFOs could get from space to Earth.[37] They also published three UFO-related news articles (two about the Condon Committee, one about a private 1998 UFO symposium), one book review, and twelve letters.

The only UFO-related empirical research paper *Science* ever published was a sociological piece, "Status Inconsistency Theory and Flying Saucer Sightings," published shortly after the AAAS symposium in 1970.[38] The paper did not consider the content or credibility of UFO reports, only the social-economic status of the people who made them.

Author Donald Warren suspected that people whose incomes didn't match their education levels—and who suffered status-related social anxiety thereby—sought to reduce their anxiety by getting attention, social recognition, and personal satisfaction through reporting a UFO sighting. Warren tested this idea against Gallup poll demographic data for people who had made UFO reports. He was wrong about the entire sample containing African-Americans, Hispanics, and white Americans. But he was right about white UFO reporters: proportionally more UFO reports came from status-inconsistent than from status-consistent white people. The report did not address the nature or credibility of the reports. It simply confirmed that if you were a white person in 1971, the more consistent your social status, the less likely you were to compromise it by reporting having seen a UFO. The establishment gatekeepers for a prestigious scientific journal took a characteristic approach to UFO evidence: don't consider what the evidence means (*what* are these

Unknowns?), but ask how it can be dismissed (*why* are these still considered Unknowns?—in this case, the theory goes, only because the reporters were social status–seekers).

Debunkers and Skeptics During the Transition

Philip Klass, the *Aviation Week* senior editor who tormented James E. McDonald, inherited Donald Menzel's role as a relentless UFO debunker. Klass attributed all UFO sightings to ball lighting, a poorly understood atmospheric phenomenon.[39] Klass wrote articles and books supporting this theory, but even Project Blue Book discounted his explanations.

Carl Sagan, a Cornell University astronomer and professor and popular science writer,[40] supported space exploration, planetary research, and the use of radio telescopes to seek electronic signals from intelligent life. Nevertheless, Sagan thought it unlikely that UFOs were extraterrestrial. In his 1974 book *Broca's Brain,* the following passage appears without a footnote or citation:

> To the best of my knowledge there are no instances out of the hundreds of thousands of UFO reports filed since 1947—not a single one—in which many people independently and reliably report a close encounter with what is clearly an alien spacecraft.[41]

Sagan was unwilling to confront UFO-related evidence. Abduction researcher Budd Hopkins and Carl Sagan met as guests on a Boston TV show in 1987. As they left the studio at the end of the show, Sagan volunteered to accompany Hopkins to study "the next really good abduction you have." Hopkins learned that a Cornell University student remembered fragments of an experience that suggested he might have been abducted. The student was willing to be interviewed by both Sagan and Hopkins. Hopkins gave Sagan the student's phone number and invited him to talk to the student first. The entire investigation would be kept confidential. A month later, Sagan wrote back to Hopkins, saying that the Cornell student's account "does not correspond to what I would call an interesting case," and declined to speak to the student or to accompany Hopkins on his meeting with the student. Sagan would not get involved, even after a promise of confidentiality and at minimum cost and effort to himself.[42]

Low, Big, and Slow

A busy person might be inclined to ignore a faraway silvery disc or cigar seen in daylight, or a distant luminous disc at night. But the UFOs reported from the mid-1960s, like some of those described in Fuller's *Incident at Exeter*, were lower, bigger, and slower than before, and harder to disregard if you happened to see one. As the twentieth century gave way to the twenty-first, the number of low, big, and slow UFO reports continued to increase.

The Taconic State Parkway Sightings

We are diurnal animals, which means that our visual system works better in daylight, we prefer to be awake during the day, and as far as night happenings are concerned, we would rather pull the covers up over our heads and forget about them. It is good that some of us are trained to work at night, because the rest of us would not be safe without the police, pilots, and other shift workers who put in hours while the rest of us are asleep. But there is still psychological resistance: if something happened after dark, it is not as much a part of the everyday world as if it happened in broad daylight. If what John G. Fuller described in *Incident at Exeter*—and what is about to be described here—had happened in broad daylight, no one would doubt the existence of extraterrestrial UFOs.

Multiple low, big, and slow UFOs were first reported in 1982 in the northern suburbs of New York City close to the Taconic State Parkway. UFO investigators were at work almost from the start. Philip Imbrogno, a high school science teacher, organized a team of local investigators associated with J. Allen Hynek's

Chicago-based Center for UFO Studies. The team tracked down leads, persuaded witnesses to report their observations, and cross-checked witnesses' accounts against local police blotters, newspapers, and other reports. Here is one of Imbrogno's witness reports from March 17, 1983:

It was about twenty minutes to nine [p.m.], and I was driving home from a church meeting in Brewster [New York]. As we approached the house I saw a large, triangular object hovering over my yard about fifty feet from my house. It seemed to be not much higher than my roof. We pulled into the driveway, and we all jumped out and ran into the backyard. The object was no longer there. I took the children into the house to get them ready for bed, but I felt a strong urge to go back outside. As soon as I left the house, I saw the object hovering over I-84, just one hundred yards or so away and twenty feet or so above a truck that was passing underneath it. I ran in and got my children and my father, and we started to watch it. It now seemed to be just above a truck that had pulled over to the side of the highway. I was amazed to see how low the object was. The traffic was stopped, and people were out of their cars looking up at it. You could see people on the bridge pointing at it. I remember saying to myself "I wish I could get a better look at it." And as I was thinking that, it made a 360-degree turn, as if rotating on a wheel, stopped, and started to float in my direction. It continued to approach me, and I just stood there transfixed. It stopped forty feet from me and was hovering twenty feet above a telephone pole in front of my house.

• • •

It was a very large, V-shaped object, a very massive size. I watched it from the time it left the I-84 until the time it

UFOs, ETs, and Alien Abductions

hovered, for approximately three minutes, and at that point all the lights seemed to intensify. . . . I watched it alone with my dad for approximately another two minutes, when we started to walk underneath it. It seemed to be about the width of a football field and was a dark, very gray metal. It was so close you could hit it with a baseball.[43]

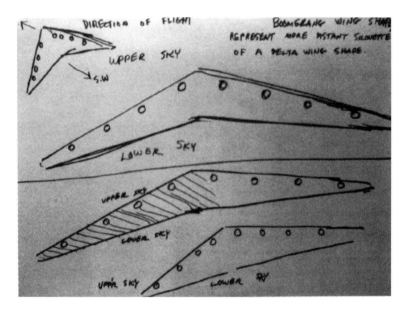

Figure 8. One of the low, big, and slow UFOs seen by hundreds of people over the Taconic State Parkway in New York State on March 24, 1983.

Imbrogno and his team gathered hundreds of additional witness reports that established a descriptive chronology from the end of 1982 to the middle of 1986, complete with photographs, of thirty-seven separate, well-corroborated, low-level nighttime appearances of giant, brightly lit, boomerang-shaped or triangular UFOs in the Taconic State Parkway region and nearby parts of New York and Connecticut. Imbrogno and his coauthors documented later sightings from the same area in the second edition of their book. Their follow-up covers cases from 1986 through 1995, many of them similar to the ones described their first edition, and the work is a tribute to their continuing dedication and perseverance. But there is a limit to what unfunded volunteers can accomplish. The entry for 1991 shows why: "Although we received many letters, due to travel plans no cases were followed up." Imbrogno's book shows the best that can be done by excellent researchers with modest private resources.

Belgium, 1989

Low, big, and slow UFOs were seen over Eupen, a small Belgian town near the German border, toward the end of 1989. The first reports described objects that looked like those seen along the Taconic State Parkway. The objects were seen at night by police, civilians, off-duty Air Force officers, and "several witnesses [who] had high-ranking functions and preferred not to reveal their names to the media." Plenty of witnesses with medium- to low-ranking functions were willing to be named, however. The government reacted quickly. They alerted the Ministry of Defence, which assigned the investigation to Wilfried De Brouwer, the chief of operations of the Air Staff.

The Belgian Air Force scrambled pairs of fighter jets on two occasions when police reported low-level sightings that were confirmed by radar. The first time the jets found nothing. The second time one of the two jets recorded a camera sequence of its radar lock-on of the UFO. Ground and airborne radar reconstruction of that jet's weaponless dogfight with the UFO showed a large object leading the jets on a chase before speeding out of sight and out of radar range. Because the other jet's radar camera had failed, the Air Force did not consider the single jet's radar camera record as definitive for the presence of an object.

The Belgian government's authoritative public report was written by General De Brouwer, who had supervised the investiga-

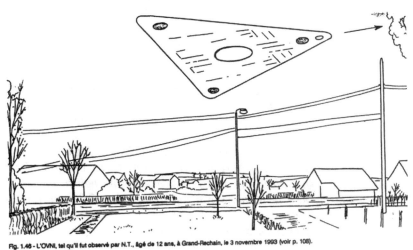

Fig. 1.46 - L'OVNI, tel qu'il fut observé par N.T., âgé de 12 ans, à Grand-Rechain, le 3 novembre 1993 (voir p. 108).

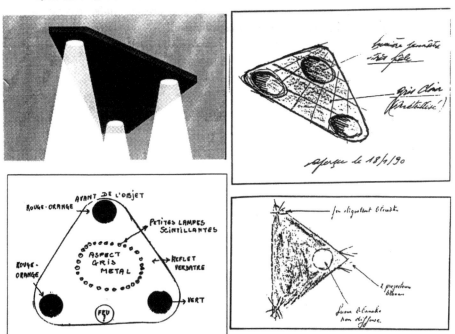

Figure 9. UFOs seen by hundreds of people over Belgium during the winter of 1989–1990.

tion. De Brouwer said his government had no interest in the complexities of the UFO problem because that was not its mandate to the Belgian people. Nevertheless, he wrote, the government wisely decided that withholding information would only make matters worse. In the end, De Brouwer released the data and concluded, with an official shrug of the shoulders, that he could not explain what had been seen in Belgian skies.

The objects seen in the Belgian experience and the Taconic State Parkway sightings were similar; but the two governments could not have responded more differently. The final answer (aside from the FAA's ludicrous "stunt flyers at night" explanation) was the same, however: the phenomena could not be explained.[44]

More Low, Big and Slow

While there are too many UFO and close-encounter cases to list them all here, observations are the foundation of both the personal and the official response to the UFO phenomenon. I have included a few more widely observed and expertly reported cases of Low, Big, and Slow UFOs to help complete a description of this persistent and transformative UFO presence over the last forty years.

Yukon Territory Event

An enormous object—much bigger than those reported near the Taconic State Parkway or in Belgium—showed up over the Yukon Territory in Canada on the clear night of December 11, 1996. This single object moved slowly enough that successive reports from witnesses at different locations established a record of its path, its size, and its speed. In contrast to the Belgian sightings, which were in a small corner of a small country, the Yukon sightings covered a large part of a large country; about 205 miles along the Klondike Highway. The UFO was seen, sometimes directly overhead and sometimes at a distance but still low in the sky, by at least thirty-one people—

Figure 10. UFO seen over Fox Lake in the Yukon Territory, Canada, in December 1996.

some along the highway near Fox Lake, others further north in the villages of Carmacks, Pelly Crossing, and Mayo.

Martin Jasek, like Philip Imbrogno, is a volunteer investigator with a day job, so his UFO travels, interviews, and reports are on his own time and at his own expense. He covered this Yukon Territory event from his home in Delta, British Columbia. Jasek talked to witnesses who told him about other witnesses. He collected individual interview reports, took witnesses to the sites of their observations, asked for position and dimension estimates, and asked them to sketch what they saw. Many of his witnesses were willing to sign their reports. Then Jasek analyzed the discrepancies among individual witness accounts, correlated witnesses' direction and dimension estimates with topographical map features of the area, and constructed an estimate of the size and appearance of the UFO by triangulation from the many observers' estimates. His computer-aided rendering of the reported UFO is shown in figure 10. The average triangulated diameter of this round UFO was nearly one mile, and its estimated height from top to bottom was one third of a mile. Witnesses who saw it overhead from the Klondike Highway estimated that it was sometimes no higher than 250 feet off the ground.[45]

Stephenville, Texas Event

A giant UFO flew low over Stephenville, Texas in January of 2008. Eyewitnesses included a constable, a chief of police, a former FAA air traffic controller, and a private pilot. Radar experts, using FAA-provided radar plots from several nearby civil airports, validated the eyewitness accounts. They confirmed that a low-flying target without a civil or military aviation transponder hovered and then flew at high speed across several Texas counties and that military jets—some fighter aircraft and some slower tracking aircraft—were diverted to and then crisscrossed the Stephenville area shortly after the UFO was seen there. The US Air Force admitted that some military jets were in the air but otherwise had nothing to say about the sighting. Neither did the FAA, except to provide the radar plots on request as required by law.

The reports and analysis describe an object that was between 500 and 1,000 feet long, observed at an altitude of between 5,000 and 17,000 feet, that sometimes flew very slowly (~50 mph) or very fast (~1,900 mph). MUFON investigators Glen Schulze and Robert Powell write "It was not any known aircraft."[46]

The End of Doubt

My favorite skeptic, R. V. Jones, would ask whether there are touch-stones that support the reliability of the data about low, big, and slow UFOs. The answer is yes. Observations were made simultaneously by multiple witnesses including police officers, military officers, and pilots. Visual sightings were correlated with ground radar plots of the objects. Fighter pilots chased objects that were observed visually and also plotted on ground radar. At least one pilot obtained an airborne radar return from a maneuvering UFO that was also painted on ground radar. The objects were larger than aircraft, and they were maneuverable.

No open-minded and reasonable person who has read and understood the evidence should now doubt that we have seen and tracked machines in our skies that we do not know how to make. It might be more accurate to say that we *have been shown* machines that we do not know how to make. Although they only appeared after dark, the big, low-flying objects reported over the Taconic State Parkway region and over small towns in Belgium, the Yukon, and Texas were not hiding: they were flaunting their presence.

PART TWO

Extraterrestrials

It is wiser, I believe, to arrive at theory by way of the evidence rather than the other way around.

—Barbara Tuchman, *Practicing History*

4

Humanoids

Now that sixty-five years of UFO evidence has been reviewed, culminating in reports of low, big, and slow objects that have been seen by hundreds of people, it should be clear that some UFOs are extraterrestrial. Do we know that some of them have crews? Yes. But first, some caveats.

Not everyone who reports a strange creature in their bedroom at night is seeing an extraterrestrial. Some people awake from sleep in the middle of the night before the inhibitory brain centers that usually prevent sleepwalking have been turned off, so they are temporarily paralyzed on awakening. If they are also awakening slowly from what is called rapid-eye-movement (REM) sleep during which people dream, they may be awake and paralyzed while their mind is still full of dream images. This so-called "hypnopompic imagery," associated with temporary paralysis, sometimes includes frightening, menacing creatures. But experiences related to the transition between sleep and wakefulness have nothing to do with UFOs.[47]

Myth, folklore, and the children's tales that spring from them are full of fairies, elves, and trolls of all kinds. They are creatures of good, mischief, or evil, depending on the tradition and on the tale. Stories of strange little beings are not new and have nothing to do with UFOs.

Public opinion about UFO occupants was tainted by the contactee movement that started in the 1950s and lasted through the 1980s.

The Master, Aura Rhanes, Alan, Lyra, or Marla from outer space never existed, and the people who believed the contactee stories of George Adamski, Truman Bethurum, Daniel Fry, Orfeo Angelucci, Howard Menger, and others (see chapter 2) were rightly thought to be self-deluded. The seeds of fact about extraterrestrial humanoids fell on ground that had been sterilized by an excess of imagination and credulity.

J. Allen Hynek Again

Acknowledging that UFOs are extraterrestrial revolutionizes our place in the universe. UFO occupant reports add an unwelcome immediacy to that revolution and produce an understandable reluctance to face it. In 1972, J. Allen Hynek wrote in *UFOs: A Scientific Inquiry*:

> To be frank, I would gladly omit this part if I could without offense to scientific integrity. . . . Unfortunately one may not omit data simply because they may not be to one's liking or in line with one's preconceived notions. . . . [W]hy should a report of a car stopped on the highway by a blinding light from an unknown craft be any different in essential strangeness or absurdity from one of a craft from which two or three little animate creatures descend?

Hynek called the occupant reports "close encounters of the third kind" (CE-IIIs). He reviewed one multiple-witness CE-III case that was reported by the Reverend William Gill, an Anglican minister in Papua New Guinea. On several June nights in 1959, Gill and many natives in the town of Boainai had low-level encounters with several UFOs seen as solid, bright objects as they moved below the low cloud cover and then as lights as they moved through and above the cloud cover. One UFO approached to an estimated 300 to 500 hundred feet above the ground, and many people saw humanoid figures in or on the UFO, who responded to a wave from some of the witnesses on the ground by waving back.

Debunker Donald Menzel said the myopic Gill had seen Venus through clouds. Gill was wearing his glasses and many of the other witnesses were not myopic.

National Investigations Committee on Aerial Phenomena (NICAP)

My first contact with occupants, so to speak, was through NICAP, which I joined in 1966. NICAP originally wanted nothing to do with occupants, contactees, or abductions. NICAP's associate director and editor Richard Hall devoted one page of the 184-page 1964 publication, *The UFO Evidence*, to occupant cases and spent most of that page reporting NICAP's exposure of a fraudulent "PhD" contactee. The book did include a drawing representing Reverend Gill's sighting, and another drawing representing the recollections of Barney Hill, one of a pair of abductees whose experiences were widely reported in John G. Fuller's 1966 book, *Interrupted Journey*. (More on Barney and Betty Hill's experience in the next chapter.)

The evidence eventually forced NICAP's hand. In 1968 I received a letter from Richard Hall and Ted Bloecher, a NICAP UFO investigator, asking me to join a fifteen-member panel to evaluate six UFO occupant reports that had originated with local NICAP committees. The panelists included John G. Fuller as well as atmospheric physicist James E. McDonald. There were aerospace medicine physicians, anthropologists, astronomers, biologists, clinical psychologists, linguists, neurologists, philosophers, research psychologists, psychiatrists, and sociologists.

I accepted NICAP's invitation and read the reports. The six cases were all from the United States. A maintenance worker saw a landed UFO in a municipal park at night. Two Navajo Indians told their close encounter story to the police. Other reporters were a dairy farmer spreading manure on a pasture, a factory worker who was hunting in the woods, an industrial draftsman who was chopping wood at an archery range, and a twenty-year-old man driving home from work. All of them reported observations of short humanoid creatures, sometimes in pairs and sometimes in groups. Most but not all of the observers were terrified by their encounter, and the people who saw them soon afterward described them as "white as a sheet" or used similar terms. No report contained enough evidence to unambiguously assess the reliability of the observers, but several reports included character witnesses. The cases reviewed by the panel were reported, among many others, in "Alien-Human Encounters," a chapter of Richard Hall's *The UFO Evidence, Volume II: A Thirty-Year Report,* published in 2001. It was the long-delayed sequel to NICAP's *The UFO Evidence, Volume I* in 1964.

My cautious opinion was that NICAP had good information about occupant sightings because NICAP's committees made good reports. I wrote that this was just the first step in establishing the reality of the occupant phenomenon. I suggested that NICAP committees should use sighting probability data to locate places where low-flying UFOs were likely to turn up and then to film or photograph them, with occupants recorded on film as a by-product. But NICAP did not survive the Condon Committee Report of 1969 long enough to collect or analyze any of the video and photographic evidence that has accumulated since then.

The observers in one of the NICAP occupant cases reported a small two-seater machine, a kind of UFO sports roadster, that has become the cartoonist's "standard model" that hovers over unsuspecting people while they are gardening or out for a walk. *The UFO Evidence, Volume II* included many independent reports of close encounters with these two-occupant vehicles, establishing them as a widely seen type along with the earlier-reported discs and cigars.[48]

The Ririe, Idaho Close Encounter

Willie Begay and Guy Tossie were twenty-three-year-old Navajo Indians who worked on a ranch near Ririe, Idaho. On November 2, 1967, they finished work and went to a local bar where they had a couple of beers, then got into their car to drive home. They had driven about a quarter-mile outside of town when a flash of white light startled and temporarily blinded them. They saw a small Saturn-shaped UFO (see figure 11) hovering about five feet off the ground in front of their car. It was about six feet in diameter and about three feet high and had a transparent bubble top through which they could see two occupants.

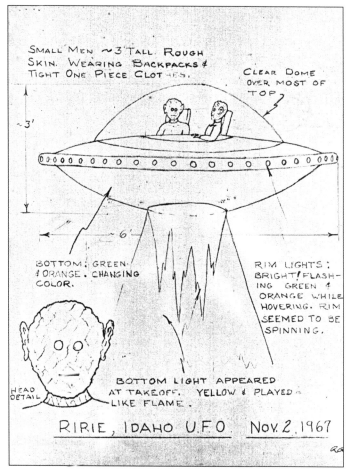

Figure 11. Sketch of the UFO and occupants seen by Willie Begay and Guy Tossie in Ririe, Idaho in November 1967.

Willie, who was driving, said the car was stopped, driven off the road, and stopped again in an adjacent field about seventy-five feet from the road without him touching the steering wheel, brakes, or accelerator. The UFO top opened and one of the small occupants floated down from the UFO, opened the driver's side door, and got in behind the steering wheel. Both men were terrified. Tossie opened the passenger side door and ran to a nearby house, where he pounded on the door until the homeowner, Guy Hammon, let him in. Meanwhile Begay slid away from the occupant behind the wheel, and, in his own words, almost passed out from fear. He said the occupant tried to talk to him with high, rapid sounds "like a woman or a bird." After a short while the occupant left the car and floated up to join the other occupant in the UFO, which "rose with a whirring sound, brightened, and flew rapidly away."

At the Hammon house, Tossie, frightened and incoherent, babbled something about a light driving their car off the road and that his friend was dead. Hammon and his son persuaded Tossie to accompany them back to the car, where they found Begay sitting in the car with his eyes closed. The car engine was running and the lights were on. Begay revived and the Indians recovered their nerves and said they would drive home.

Hammon, meanwhile, returned to the bar in Ririe to see if the bartender could shed some light on the Indians' state of mind. While he was talking to the bartender, the local constable and the county deputy sheriff came in for a sandwich. Then Begay and Tossie, who had been too afraid to drive home alone, returned to the bar for something to "settle their nerves." As soon as they saw the sheriff and constable, they rushed over to tell their story. The sheriff and constable contacted the Idaho State Police, who sent an officer to investigate. The officer found car tracks in the field but did not find marks or above-background radiation on the car. The investigator was able to locate and interview another witness who had seen an orange light, low in the sky, flying in a zigzag pattern in the same area at about the same time that evening.[49]

UFOs, ETs, and Alien Abductions

The French

In 1977 The French national space research center, Centre National d'Etudes Spatiales (CNES), established the Study Group for Unidentified Aerospace Phenomena (Groupe d'Étude des Phénomènes Aérospatiaux Non-identifiés, or GEPAN). Yves Sillard, a later director, wrote:

> The creation of GEPAN was undertaken by the CNES administration without specific instructions from the government; they thought it was their job to set up a basic, minimal organization to take account of, verify, and as far as possible explain the observations of abnormal phenomena reported by many witnesses.[50]

The group still exists. For more than thirty-five years the French government, like the Belgian government more recently, has maintained a "watching brief" over UFOs, with no attempt at secrecy and, to date, no success at explaining away those cases that are not found to be human artifacts or natural phenomena.

In the 1990s a group of former GEPAN scientists, scientific civil servants, and retired French military officers, many of them former members of the French Institute for Higher Defense Studies, formed a group called COMETA (not an acronym), which wrote a report to the French government on the UFO situation called "UFOs and Defense: What Must We Be Prepared For?" The report was not sponsored by the government but it was endorsed publicly by scientific and defense establishment insiders, and so in a way it is a 1996 version of the 1948 Estimate of the Situation that the US Air Force ultimately rejected. The difference between the two is that while French President Jacques Chirac got a copy of the COMETA report, so did anyone else who wanted one. The report concluded that the extraterrestrial hypothesis was the most plausible UFO explanation, we don't know what the ETs want, and world governments should cooperate to decide what to do about the extraterrestrials.

Among the most interesting occupant evidence cited by COMETA is a bucolic 1967 report.[51] A young boy and his sister, children of the mayor of a village on the high plateau of central France, were tending cows in a pasture on a warm and sunny day, accompanied by their dog. The dog barked to alert them that one of the cows was going AWOL over a low stone wall. The boy got up to retrieve the cow when he saw four little figures standing in a field across the road, not far from their pasture. Surprised, he called to his sister, and they both then saw a brilliant sphere near the little figures. They realized that they were not looking at children but rather at black-clad beings about four feet tall. Two of them were standing beside the sphere, one was on his knees in front of it, and the fourth held a kind of mirror which blinded the children. The boy tried to call to them, but at that instant the creatures precipitously re-entered the sphere, head first, from its top. The sphere then took off with a whistle and spiraled into the sky at great speed. The dog barked and an odor of sulfur filled the air.

Ten years later, GEPAN arranged for an official investigation. The investigators interviewed the gendarme who was called to the scene immediately after the sighting. He verified that ground traces were found where the sphere was sitting and confirmed the sulfurous smell. The fact that the children suffered for days from sore eyes was verified by their family physician. The two now-adult witnesses reconfirmed their story during the inquest. The presiding magistrate wrote in conclusion:

> Among the diverse elements of the testimony there is no discrepancy that allows us to doubt the sincerity of the witnesses, nor to postulate invention, trickery, or hallucination. Under these conditions, despite the young age of the principal witnesses, and as extraordinary as are the facts as related, I think they have been really observed.

George O'Barski and Budd Hopkins

Budd Hopkins' second career as a UFO and abduction researcher began with an occupant sighting he heard about in the Chelsea neighborhood of Manhattan, where he lived. One evening in November 1974, Hopkins crossed the street to George O'Barski's liquor store to buy a bottle of wine for dinner. He found O'Barski, whom he knew well, pacing up and down behind the counter of his small establishment, muttering to himself about life's indignities: "a man can be driving home, minding his own business, and something can come down out of the sky and scare you half to death."[52] O'Barksi's story was interrupted by other customers and by Hopkins' waiting dinner. Hopkins, his wife, and a friend had seen a UFO on Cape Cod in 1964, so Hopkins was interested enough to go back after dinner and hear the rest of O'Barski's story.

After closing the store at midnight, restocking the shelves, doing some bookkeeping, and walking his guard dog, O'Barski, a teetotaler, drove through the Lincoln Tunnel to an all-night diner in Fort Lee, New Jersey and then to his home in North Bergen. It was an unseasonably warm night in January 1974, and O'Barski's driver's side window was rolled partway down. As he drove past the east side of North Hudson Park in North Bergen, just a few hundred yards from the Hudson River, his radio picked up static; then, as he heard a humming or droning sound from outside, a brightly lit object passed his car to the left, low and over the park. O'Barski slowed as the road curved, bringing his car to within perhaps sixty feet of a thirty-foot-long craft with a row of regularly spaced, tall, narrow windows hovering just above an open field on a rise in front of him. A panel opened between two of the windows, a ladder descended, and nine or ten small figures climbed down the ladder to the ground. They were between three- and-a-half and four feet tall. Each wore an identical helmeted one-piece light-colored garment and carried a little bag and spoon-like tool with which they dug into the soil around the craft and spooned it into bags they were carrying. The creatures paid no attention as O'Barski watched them for an estimated four minutes. He saw the craft rise and fly rapidly away to the north, and then he drove on.

The next day O'Barski returned to the site, parked his car, and walked up the rise into the field, where he saw fifteen little holes, each about four to five inches deep. The holes are part of a chain of evidence that Hopkins and his UFO investigator friend Ted Bloecher assembled through a combination of diligence and good fortune. Although there were no holes in the turf when Bloecher, Hopkins, and O'Barski returned to the scene nine months after the sighting, there were fifteen little circles of dirt. Hopkins located the park custodian who told him that he had filled in the holes at the sighting location early that summer.

It was fortunate that O'Barski's sighting took place next to the Stonehenge Apartments, a cylindrical high-rise overlooking the Hudson River just to the east of the park. The Stonehenge lobby overlooked the field where O'Barski saw the UFO, and Hopkins realized that the doorman on duty that night must have seen what O'Barski saw. Hopkins, a painter and sculptor, had sold a large painting to a Stonehenge Apartment tenant in 1968. He located and interviewed the doorman, who remembered helping Hopkins deliver the painting to the tenant. The doorman said that on the night of the O'Barski sighting, at about two or three in the morning, he saw a row of ten or fifteen regularly spaced bright lights shining down from the park. He could make out a dark mass surrounding the lights. He walked over to the lobby window for a better view. As he called to alert one of the tenants to the sight, he heard a high-pitched vibration and then a sudden crack: the lobby window had broken. When he looked up again, the lights were gone. He immediately called the police about the cracked window, but he did not tell them about the lights in the park because he knew they would understand vandalism but they would not believe in UFOs. The doorman later met with Hopkins, Bloecher, and O'Barski and walked them into the park to show them where he had seen the lights. It was the same place O'Barski had seen the craft and the occupants and where there had been fifteen holes in the grass. These are the main links in a chain of additional evidence and witnesses assembled by Hopkins and Bloecher and reported on in greater detail in Hopkins' *Missing Time*.[53]

In 1976 Hopkins wrote an article about O'Barski's experience for *The Village Voice*. The article was reprinted in *Cosmopolitan* magazine a few months later. People who met Hopkins in art galleries started to tell him about their UFO sightings and close encounters. The O'Barski story thrust him into parallel careers of painter and sculptor and UFO and abduction researcher, and he made major contributions to both.

An Occupant Round Up

NICAP's 184-page *UFO Evidence, Volume I,* edited by Richard Hall in 1964, had one page about occupants. Hall's 681-page *The UFO Evidence, Volume II* published in 2001 had fifty pages about occupants and eighty pages about abductions. Volume II catalogues 107 occupant reports from 1954 to 1989. It reviews the similarities among ten of those reports that define the two-seater scout craft like the one seen by Begay and Tossie. Occupant reports are widespread; those in Volume II originate from North America, South America, Europe, Africa, and Australia. Occupant encounters are eyewitness reports corroborated by multiple witnesses (to the craft, if not the occupants, as in the O'Barski encounter) or by physical traces (as in the O'Barski encounter) or by other witnesses' attestations to the character or the physiological condition of the observers (as in the Begay and Tossie report). Most of the occupants seen through 1989 are shorter humanoids—three and one-half to four feet tall with two arms, two legs, and a head—often apparently wearing some kind of outer clothing and gear. A variety of fingers, complexions, and faces have been reported.

Willie Begay and Guy Tossie's adventure shows that some occupants have approached humans more closely and more forcefully than the humans involved either expect or want. The next three chapters are about involuntary close encounters that go even further: the "capture and release" of humans by extraterrestrials.

5

Abductions: The Index Case—
Barney and Betty Hill

The Barney and Betty Hill case is the "index case" for alien abductions. *The Interrupted Journey,* written in 1966 by John G. Fuller, and *Captured!,* written in 2007 by Stanton Friedman and Kathleen Marden, explain how the 1961 abduction experience affected Barney and Betty Hill, their immediate friends and family, and the professionals involved as the story spread through newspapers, radio, and television.[54] The Barney and Betty Hill story is the account of a sequence of dreams, emotional distress, flashbacks, physical symptoms, therapy, and hypnotically recovered memories which collectively became the first detailed description of a previously unreported human experience.

Barney Hill was an African-American World War II army veteran who became a Philadelphia postal worker and Boy Scout leader. Hill met Betty Barrett, a divorced white woman, while he was on vacation with his wife and children in New Hampshire. Barrett had taken a room in the same boarding house as the Hills while her own house was being renovated. Barney Hill eventually divorced his wife and ended up marrying Betty in 1960.

The Hills were too busy to take a honeymoon, but in September 1961 they found time for their first vacation as a married couple. Taking their dachshund Delsey with them, they drove west to

Niagara Falls, then crossed the border into Canada and drove to Toronto. They drove along the Saint Lawrence River to the Thousand Islands, and eventually on to Montreal, where they planned to stay the night. But Barney took a wrong turn in Montreal and did not understand the directions given to him by French-speaking Montrealers. They found themselves south of the city and decided to drive home, or at least back into the United States, before stopping for the night.

A Close Encounter of the Third Kind

It was September 19. Barney and Betty crossed into the United States over the Vermont border and then drove east, stopping at a restaurant in Colebrook, New Hampshire. They left the restaurant just after 10:00 p.m. The Interstates were a work in progress, so Barney drove through northern New Hampshire on US Route 3. Knowing that the road was smooth and traffic would be light, he told Betty they would be home in Portsmouth by 2:30 or 3:00 a.m. Although the night was mostly clear, a storm was moving up the east coast, giving them an incentive to get home soon. The moon was approaching full in the southern sky, Jupiter was brightly visible to the left of it, and the somewhat less bright Saturn was visible just below the moon.

South of Lancaster, New Hampshire, Betty noticed a light in the sky above Jupiter. It was bigger than the planet, and it seemed to be moving. Betty nudged Barney, who slowed the car to get a better look at it. He said that it must be a satellite. As they drove south the light was sometimes visible as the road turned and trees or mountains obstructed their view, so they found it hard to tell whether or not it was actually moving. Delsey began to get restless, a sign that she needed to go outside. When they came to a stretch of road with good visibility, Barney pulled over and stopped the car, and Betty took Delsey outside. Now that they were stopped it was clear that the light was moving. Betty gave Barney the leash and went back into the car to get the binoculars they had brought with them. They looked through them and saw more than a light.

The Hills got back into their car and continued driving. For the next twenty miles, the object played tag with them as they drove along a completely deserted section of Route 3 (now Interstate 93) through the narrow valley of Franconia Notch and past what was then the granite outline forming the Old Man of the Mountain (New Hampshire's state symbol, which fell off Cannon Mountain in 2003). They tried to make sense of what they were seeing and thought it could be a commercial airliner en route to Canada. But this theory was soon disproved by the object's sudden halts and turns. Another theory was that a light plane pilot was having fun with them. But when they stopped to look and listen, they heard no engine.

Barney and Betty passed an open motel where they might have parked, stayed the night, and ended the mystery, but instead they drove on. South of the Old Man of the Mountain and past another rock feature called Indian Head, the valley widened. The object now hovered about one hundred feet over the road in front of their car. It was a disc with a row of brightly lit rectangular windows, sixty to eighty feet in diameter and about twenty feet tall. Barney stopped the car in the middle of the road and the disc moved silently to the left and came to rest over the tree line just past the edge of a field. Barney got out of the car, bringing his binoculars with him, and walked across the field toward the disc.

Looking through the binoculars he saw a crew of black-clad figures. Suddenly all but one of them turned away from the windows toward what appeared to be an instrument panel. One figure remained looking at Barney. He felt that he was about to be captured. Betty screamed at him to come back to the car. Barney then tore the binoculars from his eyes, raced back to the car, and they drove away. As they fled, the disc moved overhead and paced them down the road.

They heard rhythmic buzzing tones coming from the car trunk. Then they heard a second set of tones. Sometime between hearing the two sets of tones Barney and Betty had unclear memories of seeing a manned roadblock and a fiery globe resting on the ground. They continued along Route 3, looking in vain for an open restaurant, until they reached Interstate 93 at Ashland and then the Route 4 turnoff to Portsmouth. They got home just after 5:00 a.m., as light streaked the eastern sky—later than the 2:30 to 3:00 a.m. arrival that Barney had predicted.

More Than a CE-III

Like the cases reported by Father William Gill, Lonnie Zamora, the French children, Willie Begay and Guy Tossie, and George O'Barski, the Hills' remembered experience was a close encounter of the third kind. What made the Hill case different, however, was what happened afterward. Barney and Betty were subdued when they arrived home. They retrieved their luggage from the car and went to sleep. When they awoke, Barney suggested that they separately draw a picture of what they had seen. They did, and the drawings were similar (Barney's is shown in figure 12).

Betty Hill's sister Janet had seen a UFO in Kingston, New Hampshire (near where the UFO reports described in *Incident at Exeter* took place). Betty called her to describe what she and Barney had seen. Janet suggested that they report their sighting to Pease Air Force Base. Meanwhile, Betty had discovered some highly polished round spots on the trunk of their car. Acting on the advice of one of Janet's physicist friends, Betty held a compass over the spots and watched as the compass needle spun round and round. It terrified her.

Betty called Pease Air Force Base and spoke to the base intelligence officer, who relayed their story completely and accurately to Project Blue Book. The accurate details were ignored by Project Blue Book, however, and the case was explained as a misidentification of an advertising searchlight.

Betty, an omnivorous reader, borrowed Donald Keyhoe's *The Flying Saucer Conspiracy* from her local library. The book included a contact address for Keyhoe's organization, NICAP, so Betty forwarded an outline of their experience to NICAP. Though NICAP was wary of "occupant" cases, Walter Webb, a local NICAP field investigator, contacted Betty, and Webb interviewed the couple in their home toward the end of October. Webb then wrote a confidential report for NICAP about the Hill sighting.

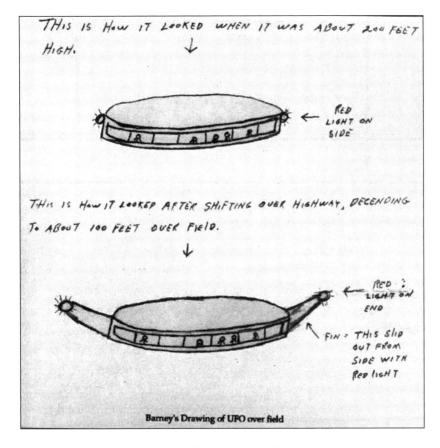

Figure 12. The UFO consciously recalled by Barney Hill after his abduction with Betty Hill in September 1961.

Shortly afterward, Keyhoe happened to be having lunch with two Boston-area IBM engineers at a Washington aeronautical conference, and he told them about the Hill sighting. The engineers wrote to the Hills and asked for another interview, and they agreed. At the end of November the Hills, the IBM engineers, and a retired Air Force intelligence major who was a friend of the Hills met for what turned out to be a five-hour meeting. The engineers noticed something that Barney and Betty already knew—they had arrived home much later than they should have, even accounting for the stop-and-go driving as they tried to figure out what they were seeing near Franconia Notch.

After the meeting, Barney and Betty recalled that Barney had made a sudden left-hand turn off Route 3 and crossed a trestle bridge. The Hills began spending some of their free time driving up and down Route 3, trying to find the turnoff and the roadblock they both vaguely remembered.

Anxiety, Nightmares, and Flashbacks

On one of these trips they came upon a stalled car partly blocking the road, surrounded by people. As Barney slowed to drive around it, Betty, terrified, implored him to drive away as fast as he could. She had to restrain herself from jumping out of the car and running away.

About ten nights after their sighting, Betty began to experience nightmares that lasted for five straight nights. The nightmares traced a continuous sequence of events that started with the conscious recollection of the first set of tones to the time when, following the second set of tones, their memory returned and they regained Route 3 and continued to drive south. They were detailed and fearful blends of her conscious memories and unfamiliar images: being stopped on a secondary road and escorted aboard a landed spacecraft, being subjected to tests, experiencing unexpected pain, being relieved of the pain, talking to some of the occupants, and being escorted back to the car with Barney and watching the spacecraft take off and fly away.

UFOs, ETs, and Alien Abductions

Barney responded sympathetically when Betty described some of these nightmares, but he did not have similar nightmares and he did not think that Betty's were anything but dreams.[55] A friend suggested that writing down the nightmares might relieve the anxiety Betty felt when she recalled them, so she wrote them down and put the notes away.

Two years after the sighting, Barney had an emotional flashback about what happened at the roadblock he and Betty had vaguely recalled seeing. Barney was with his family at the time, including Betty's niece Kathleen Marden, and as he was recounting the events of the sighting he suddenly cried out in fear as he remembered seeing men in the road who signaled him to stop the car by swinging their arms like a pendulum. Then the car motor died, and the men began walking toward the car with a swaying gait. Barney's fear was so strong that his family remembered it years afterward.

Publicity and Therapy

During another meeting at their minister's home, the Hills discussed their close encounter with Walter Webb from NICAP, their friend the retired Air Force major, the two IBM engineers who had talked with them earlier, a few people from the local community, and a few officers from Pease Air Force Base. They also talked about their close encounter to a UFO study group. Someone mentioned their story to a Boston journalist who wrote a newspaper article based on what he had heard, so their experience became more widely known in the New England area than they had anticipated.

Several people suggested that hypnosis might remove the amnesia Barney and Betty experienced between the two sets of tones. Barney also had chronic high blood pressure and stomach ulcers that were not responding to medical treatment, and his physician thought the symptoms might be psychosomatic and recommended he see a psychiatrist. With Barney's health and their shared amnesia in mind, the Hills were referred to Dr. Benjamin Simon, a Boston psychiatrist who used medical hypnosis to help soldiers suffering from combat stress (post-traumatic stress disorder) during World War II. The hypnotized soldiers were better able to remember and relive their traumatic experiences, and thereby express and purge the debilitating emotions that had been associated with them.

The Hills and Dr. Simon

The Hills' hypnosis-based therapy began near the end of 1963, about two years after their close encounter on Route 3. Dr. Simon spent several weeks training them to enter and leave a deep hypnotic trance on command to save time during the therapy sessions that would follow. He treated each of them separately in a soundproof room and tape-recorded each session.[56] He used hypnosis to help them recall what happened during their amnesic period and then he used post-hypnotic suggestion to prevent them from remembering what they had recalled under hypnosis. (This block was removed at the end of the therapy.) This meant Barney and Betty could not talk to each other about their recalled memories as the therapy progressed. Dr. Simon conducted ten separate hypnotic sessions with each of them during the first few months of 1964, concluding with post-hypnotic follow-ups that were finished by the end of June that year.

The Hills' Memories Under Hypnosis

Barney and Betty's memories, recalled separately under deep hypnosis, were like Betty's nightmares. Betty remembered becoming semiconscious as the first beeping sounds began and then trying to regain awareness after Barney suddenly drove their car off Route 3 and onto a smaller road. She willed herself back into consciousness and recalled that they were each escorted out of their stopped car by a separate group of two or three occupants. The occupants told her they just wanted to do some tests, and that they would return them to their car and let them go on their way as soon as they were finished. Betty found that her captors were too strong for her to resist

UFOs, ETs, and Alien Abductions

entering the landed disc so she eventually gave in, entered the disc by an oval door, and was taken down a corridor into a triangular-shaped room. Barney was brought into the disc behind Betty. He had not regained full consciousness and was carried into the disc dragging his feet; he remembered his shoe-tops scuffing along the ground as he was half-carried, half-floated into the craft. Betty saw that he was taken to a separate room. The occupants removed Barney and Betty's outer clothes. An occupant damaged the zipper on the back of Betty's dress and she had to finish unzipping it. Both Barney and Betty were examined by one occupant who moved between two rooms, examining each of them in turn. Barney remembered a rectal probe and a groin probe and a genital/urological probe. The examiner used needles connected to wires to probe his skin and then examined and took samples from Barney's ears and skin. The occupants inspected Barney and Betty's mouths and were surprised to find that Barney had removable teeth (dentures) and Betty did not. Barney also remembered looking into the examiner's mouth as the examiner was bending over him and seeing a membrane that moved when the examiner made *mmm-mmm-mmm* sounds that seemed to be directed toward other occupants in the room.

There was another occupant in Betty's examination room whom she called the "leader." Although he made sounds that were not English words, she understood them as if they were in English. She could also understand some of what the examiner said in the same way. After the leader told her it would not hurt, the examiner inserted a large needle in Betty's navel. It hurt badly, apparently surprising the examiner and the leader. The leader waved his hand over Betty's face, and the pain went away.

When the examiner left the room to examine Barney, Betty was left alone with the leader. She felt more at ease since the examination was over, and they had a conversation. Betty said she was astonished at their encounter and opined that it would be hard to convince anyone that it had happened. She said she would like to take a souvenir with them, and the leader looked around and asked her what she would like to take. She saw something like a book lying on a cabinet and asked if she could take it. The leader asked if she could read it. She said she couldn't, but that did not matter; the book was simply a proof of their meeting. The leader agreed. Then she asked him where they were from. He asked her if she knew much about the universe, and after she told him what very little she did know, he opened a star map. Betty recalled afterward that it was perhaps three feet wide, oblong, and almost self-luminous, like a holographic projection. It showed bright circles of various sizes connected by solid lines between larger circles and some dotted lines. She was told that the circles represented stars or planets, the lines represented trade routes, and the dotted lines represented expeditions. The leader asked her if she knew where she was on this map, and she said no. At which point the leader said, "If you don't know where you are, there wouldn't be any point in me telling you where I am,"[57] and he closed the map.

Barney was escorted back to their car while Betty was talking to the leader. As she was preparing to leave, a commotion arose among the crew. A single occupant who was shorter, rounder-faced, and apparently angrier than the others, and who seemed to Betty to be in a position of authority, objected to giving Betty the book and she was forced to give it back. The leader also said they had decided to prevent Barney and Betty from remembering what had happened to them. The leader said even if Betty remembered anything Barney would not, or if he did, his memories would contradict hers and they would end up totally confused.

Betty returned to the car where Barney was already sitting behind the wheel and Delsey the dachshund had been left during the abduction. They sat in the car and watched the disc take on an orange glow, lift into the sky, and disappear from view. Barney started the car and maneuvered back down the road and rejoined the concrete pavement of Route 3. Then the second set of beeping tones occurred, and they regained full memory near Interstate 93 at Ashland. They drove down I-93 until they reached Route 4, turned east on Route 4, and drove home to Portsmouth.

Dr. Simon's Explanation

Dr. Simon never endorsed the reality of Barney and Betty Hill's abduction experience, but he did admit that he could not explain much of what the Hills told him during their hypnosis sessions. He did not know where Betty's nightmares came from, nor did he have an explanation for why they matched her recovered memories.[58] Dr. Simon was skeptical, however, of Barney's story. He knew that Betty had told Barney about her nightmares and suggested that Barney was "filling in" with information he had remembered hearing from Betty.

Although the therapy led to partial relief of Barney's symptoms, the Hills were disappointed that Dr. Simon would not say that the experience was real. Nevertheless Barney and Betty remained in touch with him and he remained willing, when given the Hills' permission, to talk about their experiences and his role in the case. Dr. Simon did believe that Barney and Betty had experienced a close encounter of the third kind (CE-III) and spoke to J. Allen Hynek and a few other UFO researchers about it.

Physical Evidence

There is more to the Barney and Betty Hill case than their stories; there is the physical evidence that supports their story. First are the polished circles on the trunk of the Hills' car that made a compass needle spin when placed on top of them. The spots gradually faded away after a year but were seen by many witnesses, including Betty's niece Kathleen Marden. The Hills believed these spots were associated with the two sets of tones they heard at the beginning and end of their amnesic period.

Second, there is the broken binocular strap. Barney remembers tearing the binoculars from his eyes and racing back to the car when he felt that they were about to be captured; the strap probably broke then.

Third, both Barney and Betty's mechanical wristwatches stopped working after the trip and could never be made to work again.

Fourth, there is Betty's dress. When the Hills got back from their trip, Betty took the dress off, hung it in a closet, and never wore it again. When the dress was inspected later, the lining was ripped and there were tears in the threads holding the zipper in place. This damage is consistent with the memory that an occupant could not manipulate the zipper, got it stuck, and Betty had to finish unzipping it.

Fifth, Barney's shoe-tops were scuffed, as if they had been dragged along the ground. They would not scuff on top as a result of normal walking. The scuffed shoe-tops are consistent with Betty's memory that Barney was dragged into the landed disc by two occupants.

Sixth, after the sighting, Barney developed a circle of twenty-one three-quarter-inch warts on his groin. He remembered under hypnosis that some kind of probe or instrument had been placed against his skin. They were not venereal warts and in fact seemed to be a benign if ugly growth, and Barney eventually had them removed.

The seventh, and certainly the strangest, piece of physical evidence was the return of Betty's earrings. A few weeks after their encounter, the Hills locked up their house and left on a day trip up Route 3 to look for the landing site. They returned that evening, unlocked the house, and found a pile of dried leaves on the kitchen table. The earrings that Betty had worn on the September journey were in the middle of the pile. She had missed them but had not done anything about it.

Dr. Simon reminded them that if they had been abducted, it must have happened somewhere. They had not found the location after their first few day trips, but eventually they turned off Route 3 and crossed a trestle bridge that they remembered seeing on the night of the abduction, turned up a narrow dirt track off the secondary road, and came to a clearing that they both recalled as being the abduction site.

Correlations

After the Hills' story was published two of Betty's remembered experiences were followed up on by investigations. First, Betty remembered under hypnosis the star map she had been shown by the leader, and her post-hypnotic drawing was published in *The Interrupted Journey*. Amateur astronomer Marjorie Fish, a teacher and MENSA member, saw Betty's drawing and created a three-dimensional model to try to find out if Betty's map matched up to our galaxy. She located all of the stars within fifty-five light-years of the sun by reviewing printed star catalogs, and she used different sizes and colors of beads to represent different types of stars. The beads were suspended using nylon fishing line. Her three-dimensional construction began in 1968 and evolved as new and more accurate star data was obtained and published. In 1972, using data from the most recently published catalog, she found a single position from which the Betty Hill two-dimensional star map superimposed itself accurately on the sun-like stars in her three-dimensional map. She identified the two main stars on Betty Hill's remembered map as Zeta 1 and Zeta 2 Reticuli, and found that one of the stars joined to the pair of main stars by lines in the Betty Hill map was our sun.

Second, during her abduction, Betty had been offered a souvenir book by the leader, but another occupant overruled that decision and Betty was forced to leave the craft without it. Betty later drew the symbols she remembered seeing on the book, and in 2007 her drawing was published for the first time in *Captured!* UFO researcher Budd Hopkins had collected drawings over many years from abductees who said they remembered seeing symbols inside a craft. The symbols Betty remembered and that were published for the first time in 2007 look remarkably like many of the symbols that Hopkins had been collecting from abductees since 1975 (see figure 3 on page xxi and figure 13 on page 100).[59]

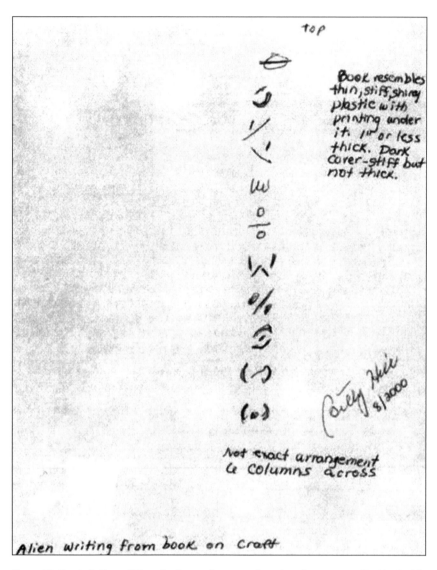

Figure 13. Symbols Betty Hill, under hypnosis, remembered seeing on a small tablet inside the UFO during their abduction.

UFOs, ETs, and Alien Abductions

The Aftermath

The publicity and travel associated with the publication of *Interrupted Journey* moved Barney and Betty's lives out of the ordinary but did not totally dominate them. The Hills remained socially and politically active in areas having nothing to do with UFOs after their encounter. They were active in the NAACP, the Unitarian church, and politics. They went to Lyndon Johnson's inauguration in 1965 as part of the New Hampshire Democratic Party delegation. Barney was appointed to the New Hampshire State Advisory Committee on Human Rights, a branch of the United States Commission on Human Rights, in the same year. Betty rented apartments in their renovated house to servicemen stationed at Pease Air Force Base in Portsmouth, and the Hills socialized with their tenants and other service families at the Officers' Club and Families' Club on the Air Force base. In 1969, Barney died unexpectedly of a stroke.

After Barney's death, Betty began to spend more of her time looking for UFOs, talking to people about them, and seeing them—sometimes verifiably, sometimes with more imagination than common sense. She became a fixture on the UFO lecture circuit. Friends including John G. Fuller, author of *Interrupted Journey,* urged her to be cautious about reporting more UFOs, but for many years she went her own way. She eventually tired of the UFO circuit, perhaps realizing that she and others may have had more enthusiasm than data. Pease Air Force Base closed in 1991, and the friends she had maintained in that community left with it. Betty remained close to her family and a few friends who supported her warmly as her health declined until she died of lung cancer in 2004.

Conclusion

Barney and Betty Hill's account offers evidence that humans have been involuntarily taken aboard an extraterrestrial vehicle, examined, and returned; in other words, that humans have been abducted by aliens. If this were an isolated case, it would remain an anomaly with no conventional explanation. The combination of consciously remembered experience, physical evidence, nightmares, flashbacks, and memories recalled under hypnosis might have been a complex joke arranged by Coincidence to baffle humans. But this was not an isolated case: it was a documented precursor to many others.

Return for a moment to R. V. Jones' valuable intelligence lesson about finding a touchstone to distinguish reliable from unreliable reports. Here are some touchstones we might expect to see in an abduction narrative: conscious recollection of a close encounter; missing time; anxiety about the experience; flashbacks or dreams with an abduction theme; and finally, if the dreams or flashbacks are incomplete, aided recall of the abduction experience with the caveat that the professional involved is competent and unbiased.

Consider the following characteristics of the Barney and Betty Hill case:

1. There was conscious recollection of a CE-III.

2. There was a period of missing time.

3. There was physical evidence in the form of spots on the car, scuffed shoes, torn clothing, and Barney's groin warts.

4. There were nightmares and flashbacks about an abduction experience.

5. Memory recalled under hypnosis accounted for the period of missing time.

If CE-IIIs followed by abductions are a consistent phenomenon and not an anomaly that common sense tells us to ignore, then there should be more accounts like this from reliable observers analyzed by competent researchers. There are.

6

Abductions:
The Touchstone Cases

A reasonable person should not rush to judgment after reading the Barney and Betty Hill index case. One case with no precedent may stimulate interest in the abduction experience, but by itself it should not justify a change of opinion. More information, and consistent information, is needed to establish the reliable and repeatable aspects of the phenomenon. The five cases presented in this chapter all include what R. V. Jones called "touchstones": credible, repeated facts that strengthen confidence that the reports form a consistent basis for understanding the abduction phenomenon.

Encounter at Buff Ledge

On the evening of August 7, 1968, two camp counselors were abducted from the Buff Ledge Camp on the eastern shore of Lake Champlain near Burlington, Vermont.[60] Most of the Buff Ledge campers and staff had gone to an event in Burlington that day, and the waterfront was deserted. Two of the employees, Michael Lapp and Janet Cornell (not their real names), put on bathing suits and went down to the dock to talk and swim.

Their consciously recalled UFO sighting began after sunset at about 8:10 p.m. They noticed a bright star-like object in the southwestern sky. Michael thought it was Venus until it swung down from its position in a long arc to the right, moving perhaps fifty degrees in a few seconds. When it stopped it looked large, cigar-shaped, and self-luminous.

Three small lights emerged from the end of the object. The lights carried out a series of visually compelling maneuvers, spiraling upward, fluttering downward, and eventually appearing as luminous discs as they moved closer to Michael and Janet. Two of the disks departed abruptly, and the third, making a sound like many tuning forks, abruptly rose and then plunged into the lake, creating whitecaps and wind that persisted until it suddenly rose out of the water a few minutes later and moved over the lake to approach the end of the dock where Michael and Janet stood, both of them in awe. The disc that hovered near them appeared "as big as a small house"—Michael estimated that it was forty to fifty feet in diameter—and had a transparent dome on top through which they could see two occupants.

Janet was stunned. Michael turned to the figures in the UFO and said out loud: "What do you want? Where are you from? Are you going to hurt us?" and to his surprise a voice answered (in his head): "We are not here to harm you." Michael and the occupant carried out a conversation in which he spoke out loud but the occupant's part was "telepathic." Janet remained incommunicado.

Eventually the UFO hovered above and directly over the dock and shone down a bright light that enveloped the two of them. Michael lost consciousness. When he regained consciousness it was about 9:00 p.m. and he heard the sound of car doors slamming as campers returned from Burlington. Two of the returning campers saw lights over the dock, ran down to the water's edge to see what was happening, and saw the UFO disappear into the night. A staff member saw the UFO from an upstairs window of the camp's main building.

Neither Michael nor Janet ever publicized or exploited their involvement in a UFO close encounter/abduction case. Years later Michael, who still lived in Vermont, decided to explore the experience he had not forgotten but had never resolved. He called

J. Allen Hynek's Center for UFO Studies in Chicago, and they referred him to Walter Webb, the NICAP field investigator who first interviewed Barney and Betty Hill. Webb, an astronomer, was for thirty-two years a senior lecturer, assistant director, and operations manager of the Charles Hayden Planetarium at the Museum of Science in Boston.

Webb invited Lapp to Boston and interviewed him for seven hours. Lapp remembered witness Janet Cornell and the other campers who saw the UFO, but where were they now? Lapp and Cornell had not met nor been in contact since the summer of 1968. Michael found Janet's current business address, Webb wrote her a letter, and she called back. Her memory of the shared experience was not as detailed as Michael's, but it did include a period of "missing time" when the bright light hovered over the dock. Although Janet had chosen to disregard the experience, she was willing to undergo hypnosis to discover what she could not remember during her "missing time."

At Webb's suggestion, Michael and Janet agreed to be hypnotized to try and learn what had happened during their "missing time." Michael thought it was a good idea from the start, and Janet was encouraged by her husband. Although Janet lived in Atlanta, she returned routinely to the Boston area on business, so it was possible to arrange hypnosis sessions with Boston-area hypnotherapists who volunteered their services. Michael was interviewed a total of five times by two therapists and Janet was interviewed separately, twice, by one therapist. During this time Lapp and Cornell only met once, for two hours at Boston's Logan Airport while Janet was waiting for a connecting flight. Michael had completed one hypnosis session by then and Janet had not yet started hers, but Webb, who was there, made sure nothing that Michael described during his hypnosis session was discussed at their meeting. Webb was present at all the interviews. Unlike Dr. Simon, the therapists did not block Michael or Janet's later recall of what they remembered during hypnosis.

Michael and Janet's conscious and hypnotically recalled memories agree that they were standing on the dock directly under the

UFO when an intense beam of white light shone down on them. Michael remembered pushing Janet and himself to the ground, and that is where their conscious memories ended. Under hypnosis, they remembered being floated up the beam of light and into the transparent dome of the UFO, where they joined four occupants. The occupants were short, had greenish-blue skin, large heads, thin necks, large, goggly, protruding eyes, small or rudimentary ears and nose, and small mouths, and their hands appeared to have three long fingers. They appeared to be wearing skin-tight, silver-gray clothing. They communicated with each other through a high-pitched, continuous sound but communicated with Michael and Janet telepathically, mostly to reassure them that they would not be hurt. Michael and Janet were examined on a tilting examination table. Michael remembers little of his own exam but remembers seeing Janet's examination, part of which she also remembers. He and she both remember probes being placed at various parts of their bodies.

Michael remembered that the UFO over the dock rendezvoused with a very large ship, possibly the one they had seen first. When he looked through the transparent dome as they approached the large ship, he could see the Earth the size of "a nickel at arm's length" and the moon to the side. Webb estimated that the observation point might have been about 200,000 miles from Earth. The smaller UFO entered a hangar inside the larger ship and Michael and Janet floated down a "light tunnel" that joined their smaller ship to a door in the hangar wall. Janet had far less detailed memories of the larger ship, but Michael remembered a confusing scenario of humans, some clothed, some naked, congregating in a misty outdoors environment. His memories of what followed were not resolved, but he also remembered seeing display screens that presented rapidly changing information continuously, and he was told that he was learning it for use in the future. Finally, he remembers seeing an image projected on the screens of he and Janet lying on the dock, at which point his conscious memory returned and he found himself back on the dock.

After following many leads, writing many letters, and making many phone calls Webb was able to find all of the witnesses that Michael remembered, as well as several more ex-campers and ex-counselors who also saw the mysterious lights over the dock. By the time Walter Webb published *Encounter at Buff Ledge*, Michael Lapp had graduated from college with a bachelor's degree. Janet Cornell, three years older than Lapp, had graduated from college, earned a masters' degree *summa cum laude*, found professional work, become the wife of a physician, and then a mother.

The West Nyack, New York Incident

Missing Time, written by Budd Hopkins and published in 1981, was the first book since *Interrupted Journey* to report abductions to a wide audience. Appropriately enough, an important piece of evidence in the following *Missing Time* case was a "missing time" entry on the police blotter in Clarkstown, New York, on Friday, April 5, 1969.

Denis McMahon, Paul Federico, and Douglas Sharkey, all seventeen years old, met shortly after dinner on Friday evening (at the latest, 7:30 p.m.), as was their custom, and drove in McMahon's car to a road overlooking DeForest Lake, just north of West Nyack, New York. West Nyack is on the west side of the Hudson River about twenty miles north of New York City, close to the New Jersey state line. They parked and talked about what they planned to do for the rest of the evening, which by parental order had to end by 11:00 p.m.

While they were talking, one of them noticed a light reflecting off the top of the dashboard. McMahon got out of the car to see what it was and found himself looking up at the bottom of a UFO hovering above a nearby telephone pole. It was about fifty feet in diameter. A beam of light was shining down from its center, and red and white lights were revolving around its outer edge. McMahon remembered that he tried to start the car, but it wouldn't start even though it had a new battery. He waited a few minutes and tried to start it again, and this time it did start. The boys drove to nearby Clarkstown to report the incident—their second report in one week. The previous Friday, the boys, along with many other people, including policemen, had seen a low-flying UFO moving along the railroad tracks in nearby Pearl River, New York.

Ten years after the incident in West Nyack, Budd Hopkins was the guest on a radio talk show about UFOs, and McMahon called in to describe his sighting. Hopkins met with McMahon and Federico at DeForest Lake soon after the call. He reminded them that they said they had seen the UFO shortly after parking their car near DeForest Lake and had then driven to the police station and made their report as soon as McMahon could start the car. Hopkins retrieved the police incident report. It was recorded at 10:23 p.m.

If the boys had arrived at the DeForest Lake location at about 7:30 p.m., as they usually did, and if they had seen the UFO at about 8:00 p.m. or "shortly after" and had driven as soon as possible afterward to the police station, then there was a period of missing time from about 8:00 to 10:00 p.m., given that it took at most fifteen minutes to drive from the sighting location to the Clarkstown Police Station.

NBC was making a UFO documentary with Hopkins' help when McMahon called into the radio show, and the producer of the documentary invited McMahon and Federico to return to the DeForest Lake location for a video reenactment of their close encounter. (The third witness, Douglas Sharkey, was not located.) While they were at the site with the film crews, Paul Federico remembered having had a dream about the sighting. He dreamed that the UFO had landed and it had stayed about twenty minutes. During that time it shone its beam on him, which made him feel very relaxed and very calm, "almost as if I were in my mother's arms as a little baby." After seeing the completed series on TV, Denis McMahon and his girlfriend were driving home late one evening when he had a flashback about the close encounter. He told Hopkins, "I just started remembering a lot of stuff, and I started talking to her [McMahon's girlfriend], and I almost went to tears. I almost went to pieces. I was driving the car and talking and everything was just flowing out . . . and I started to shake."

McMahon recalled being drawn into the UFO by the beam of light and then being placed on a table and examined by at least three humanoid occupants who were four-and-one-half to five feet tall, had pale grayish skin, large black eyes, and appeared to be wearing skintight clothing about the same color as their skin. McMahon was frightened. He said the occupants were silent and dispassionate and he "felt like a worm on a hook."

McMahon's recall of the abduction and examination was spontaneous and emotional. Successive recall attempts often lead to more accurate recall, even if the forgotten information is not recalled on the first try,[61] and McMahon's recall was triggered when he called the radio talk show and described his close encounter. Meeting with Hopkins, staging the on-site reenactment with the TV crew, and then seeing the three-part program that aired shortly afterward further helped him recall his experience. The program did not describe UFO interiors or examinations, so it could not have been a source of material for a fantasy abduction and examination. Federico's dream, while less detailed, also extended beyond the consciously remembered sighting and added an emotional tone that was different from McMahon's recall.

Ten years after the close encounter and abduction, Federico and McMahon were gainfully and respectably employed. Although their names had been used on the NBC documentary, they neither sought nor benefited from publicity following their experience.

The McMahon-Federico experience has elements in common with those of Barney and Betty Hill and of Michael Lapp and Janet Cornell. There was conscious recall of a close encounter, conscious awareness of missing time, and emotional aftereffects. The abduction was recalled in a dream by Betty Hill and Paul Federico. The abduction was recalled under hypnosis independently by Barney and Betty Hill and independently by Michael Lapp and Janet Cornell. The abduction was recalled without hypnosis by Denis McMahon. The touchstones to this very odd human experience are the conscious recall of a close encounter and the conscious recall of missing time. Then the abduction was recalled either spontaneously, as with McMahon, or following a hypnotic suggestion to remember.

The Allagash Abduction

If two witnesses are good, four should be better—especially when all four have talents that enable them to transform memories into narrative and image.[62] Four such friends from New England went on a weeklong trip to northern Maine in August, 1976. Jack Weiner had a BFA from the Massachusetts College of Arts. Jim Weiner, Jack's twin brother, had a BA in psychology and was studying ceramics. Charlie Foltz also had a BFA, and Chuck Rak had attended the same college but did not have a degree. They left Boston by car on Saturday, August 20 and headed for Baxter State Park in Maine. First they climbed Mount Katahdin. Their next stop was the Allagash Wilderness Waterway, a 92-mile chain of lakes, ponds, and rivers. On Monday, August 23 they landed by floatplane on Telos Lake. Like all visitors to the Allagash, they were registered by the local park ranger. By Tuesday evening they had canoed through Telos Lake and were settling in at a campsite on the south shore of Chamberlain Lake.

On that practically moonless night another camper pointed to an intense bright light low on the eastern sky. Jim Weiner, the ceramics student, wrote, "The light was most peculiar. It resembled that quality of light one sees inside a pottery kiln at cone 10, approximately 2,350° Fahrenheit." Through binoculars it looked as if it were just a few miles away and a few hundred feet above treetop level. The light disappeared after a few seconds, and in the business of setting up camp, as soon as the nocturnal light (NL) was out of sight it was also out of mind.

They spent a rainy Wednesday in camp on Chamberlain Lake. On Thursday morning they got into their canoe and paddled from Chamberlain Lake to Eagle Lake, where they pitched their tent at a deserted campsite near Smith Brook. They spent the afternoon fishing, without luck. They returned to camp and ate their last fresh food for dinner, then resolved to try their fishing luck again after dark. They built a beacon fire at the campsite large enough to burn for two or three hours, so in the absence of a moon they could find their way back to camp. All four set off again in one canoe.

As they were paddling across the water, they saw a fiery sphere rise from behind the trees on the other side of Eagle Lake. As Chuck Rak described it:

> I could see a fluid pulsating over the face of the object as it changed color from red to green to yellow-white. As my eyes became adapted to the intense brightness, I detected a gyroscopic motion, as if there were pathways of energy flowing equatorially and longitudinally from pole to pole. They divided the sphere into four oscillating quadrants of bright colored light. The color changes were very liquid and enveloping as if the entire object had a plasmic motion to it like a thick sauce does as it starts a rolling boil.

Jack Weiner saw "a very large, pulsating, spherical light. It was not making any noise at all" and it looked "as big as a house, at least eighty feet in diameter." Jim Weiner said he immediately recognized it as the same light they had seen from the campsite on Chamberlain Lake. Charlie Foltz said "I was holding a large flashlight which I then flashed at the sphere—three short, three long and three short flashes [SOS]."

As soon as Charlie flashed his SOS, the sphere moved toward the canoe. They hesitated momentarily, then started paddling to shore. Two of them remembered that the sphere hovered directly over the canoe and enveloped them in a cone-shaped beam of white light. The next thing they all remember was that they were out of their canoe and standing on the shore at their campsite, watching the sphere hover over the water about fifty yards from shore. The beam of light suddenly turned away from the water and pointed toward the sky, and then the sphere sped away at a tremendous speed and disappeared.

Jim Weiner said "we all seemed to be in a state of shock, because, for a few minutes, we just stood there unable to move or talk. . . . The entire experience seemed to last, at the most, fifteen or twenty minutes. Yet the fire was completely burned down to red coals!" They fell asleep around the picnic table at the campsite. The next day, they broke camp and paddled on to the next campsite in the chain of lakes. They told the forest ranger they met at that campsite about their sighting but he did not take it seriously. The diaries that the four campers had kept before the sighting petered out and they said later that they remembered little of the last few days of their trip.

Ten years after the close encounter, Jack Weiner started to have recurring nightmares. He dreamed of being in a bright, hazy space where he could see the three other Allagash campers sitting on a bench near him. Two creatures came out of the haze and started to examine him. One held a metallic probe in a claw-like hand. Jack panicked and woke in a cold sweat. His fear persisted for days. When the nightmares began he could not see the creatures' faces, but as the nightmares persisted their faces became clearer and he could remember and draw what he had seen.

Jim Weiner also reported troubling nighttime experiences. Jack and Jim had kept in touch with Chuck Rak and Charlie Foltz, and Jim knew that the other Allagash campers were also having nightmares.

Ron Brown, a clinical psychology doctoral student at my university, studied the function of dreams. Brown compared the dream content and mental state of people who were experiencing recurring dreams with those whose recurring dreams had stopped at least six months earlier as well as those who had never experienced recurring dreams.[63] He discovered that recurring dreams indicate unresolved psychological conflict, and when the conflict is resolved the recurring dreams stop and the person begins to feel better. As Brown learned through his research and the Allagash campers knew by experience, nightmares mean unresolved psychological conflicts, and unresolved conflicts mean a diminished sense of well-being.

Figure 14. Drawing of UFO occupants remembered by Charlie Foltz, one of the Allagash abductees.

Figure 15. Charlie Foltz's drawing of occupants examining another abductee aboard the UFO.

In 1988, Jim Weiner attended a Boston-area UFO meeting to talk to people who might know something about the aftereffects of a close encounter. Raymond Fowler, the eventual author of *The Allagash Abductions*, was there. Ray listened to Jim's story, noting his surprise when he recounted returning to a completely burned-down fire after what was remembered as a fifteen-to-twenty-minute-long close encounter. Fowler arranged interviews and hypnotic interventions with all four of the Allagash campers based on their interest, their accessibility (all still lived in New England), and their shared experience of missing time. The interviews and interventions were separate for each of them, but the therapist allowed them to remember what they recalled under hypnosis.

The four narratives that emerged from the hypnosis sessions were complementary and consistent, and by now the story will not surprise you. All four witnesses remembered being levitated, one by one, out of the canoe, up inside the hollow cone of light and into the sphere. Each of the campers remembered encountering three or four occupants, and they illustrated their memories with drawings that were consistent with Jim Weiner's occupant drawings based on his nightmares (see figures 14 and 15). They remembered being told telepathically what they had to do. Jim remembered Jack being examined by several occupants (as in his nightmare), and he remembered being taken to another room and examined on a table. He was made to produce a sperm sample.

Each of them remembered seeing the others in the sphere, and each of them remembered being examined in turn. They remembered sitting together on a bench waiting for the others' examinations to finish. Jim Weiner was made to get into a machine that terrified him because it made his body feel like it was coming apart; the next thing he remembered was being back in the canoe. The others' memories of returning to the canoe were less clear and less traumatic. When they were levitated out of their canoe it was about 1,000 feet from shore, but when they were returned to it, it was only forty or fifty feet from their campsite.

The quality of the Allagash witnesses' drawings puts this abduction narrative into a class by itself. What I have summarized here is only the "conventional"—if that word is even imaginable in this context—part of the abduction experience. It does not include many events, some consciously remembered and some remembered under hypnosis, that all four of the abductees experienced either before or after the abduction. The rest of the story is told in *The Allagash Abductions*.

UFO Abduction Near Goodland, Kansas

I know, patient reader, that tedium can grow over a succession of "a man walking his dog and a police officer in a patrol car saw a . . ." reports. Nevertheless, I want to show you that UFO close encounter reports are as consistent as UFO reports. The next case was reported in the *Journal of UFO Studies,* a peer-reviewed scientific journal that reports evidence, criticism, and ideas about UFO and abduction phenomena.[64] I have met the witnesses and the reporter of this next account. They are gainfully employed middle-class people.

Susan and Jennifer (not their real names) were driving east along Interstate 70 in Colorado on their way home to St. Louis, Missouri on the night of November 7, 1989. They were returning from a conference in Aspen and were planning to drive as far as Goodland, Kansas before stopping for the night. They stopped for gas in Flagler, Colorado at about 11:30 p.m. Driving seventy-five to eighty miles per hour, they expected to cross the seventy-two miles between Flagler and Goodland in about an hour.

Just after leaving Flagler they noticed a bright object very high in the sky that kept a constant position relative to their car. It occasionally moved with little jerks and stops. They saw flashing, colored lights on it, and they noticed some small green lights near it. They kept the object in view (and the object kept them in view) for almost an hour. The dashboard clock read 12:40 a.m. when they pulled off the road and dimmed their lights to get a better look at the object. A ball of light suddenly dropped down and hovered over a field within one hundred feet of their car. It shone a cone of light with pastel-colored rays that reached toward the ground, and they saw what looked like heat waves rising from the ground near the light cone. Susan started the car and pulled back onto the road, and after the excitement and adrenalin rush of the close encounter they both felt exhausted and irritable. They arrived a few minutes later at Goodland, found a motel, and checked in—at 2:30 in the morning.

They experienced the by now familiar constellation of signs: a close encounter, missing time, and emotional changes. The follow-up was also familiar. Jennifer had disturbed sleep and nosebleeds. Susan was upset enough to contact the local chapter of MUFON for information about UFOs and help in resolving their missing time. Susan was interested in hypnosis, so MUFON put her in touch with John Carpenter, a psychotherapist who uses hypnosis in his practice. Carpenter contacted Jennifer through Susan and arranged separate hypnosis sessions with each of them. Jennifer and Susan were asked to not talk to each other until after the sessions were finished, and they agreed.

Under hypnosis, they each independently recalled being levitated up through a cone of light that enveloped their car. They remembered being examined by occupants similar in size and appearance to those described by the Allagash abductees. Susan remembered watching Jennifer's examination and Jennifer remembers being examined, but Jennifer did not remember seeing Susan being examined. Susan remembered being told telepathically that this was being done for their mutual benefit. They drew sketches of the UFO and the occupants, and both the occupants and the interiors were similar. Jennifer also remembered seeing slightly shorter occupants with large eyes and small suction cups on their fingertips. They remember being levitated back down to their car, and as they re-entered the car, they started to forget the abduction experience.

The investigation showed that, as with the Allagash abductees, both Susan and Jennifer had experienced more than one encounter with the same or similar occupants. Neither witness has sought or received publicity or recognition for their experience, which was reported only in the *Journal of UFO Studies*, at a UFO conference,[65] and in secondary sources. With the exception of Betty Hill, none of the abductees whose accounts have been presented here ever became part of a UFO community. They are ordinary Americans with well-documented histories of extraterrestrial intrusion into their daily and nightly lives.

New York City UFO Abduction

Two American security officers and the diplomat they were protecting saw a woman being abducted into a UFO from an apartment building in downtown Manhattan. It happened on the night of November 30, 1989—three weeks after Susan and Jennifer were abducted near Goodland, Kansas. I met the abductee, Linda Cortile (not her real name), under conditions that persuaded me that the abduction experience had a powerful emotional impact. My account is based on Linda Cortile's conscious memories, my discussions with her and other witnesses, her hypnotically induced recall, and Hopkins' book, *Witnessed: The True Story of the Brooklyn Bridge UFO Abductions.*

Budd Hopkins' *Intruders: The Incredible Visitations at Copley Woods*, published in 1987, was about an abduction in a neighborhood near Indianapolis, Indiana. *Intruders*, like *Missing Time*, was a popular book that publicized both the abduction experience and Hopkins' interest in it. The last page was captioned: "How to Report a Suspected UFO Experience." One choice was to contact Hopkins through his publisher, Random House, and an address was provided.

Linda Cortile is the first-generation daughter of Italian immigrants and has lived in New York City all her life. She had read *Intruders*, and in April 1989 she wrote to Hopkins describing experiences that had begun in her parents' home while she was living there as a young adult and that persisted after she married and left home.

After going to bed, instead of falling asleep she would sometimes find herself becoming numb from her feet to her neck. Although she kept her eyes closed, she had images of shrouded, hooded figures around her bed. She sometimes cried out as the experience started, but her parents (and later her husband) never heard her cries. Gradually the numbness would recede, and she would wait for morning. She did not know what had happened and was reluctant to talk about what she did remember. Her parents dismissed her experiences as nightmares. Her husband tried to comfort her but only ended up worrying about her. Doctors found nothing wrong; happily married with a young son, Linda had no troubles that would have brought on a psychosomatic illness.

In May 1989 Linda met with Hopkins to discuss her experiences. When she was eight years old she remembered seeing a brightly lit object hovering over a nearby apartment building. Hopkins induced hypnosis, and Linda recalled more clearly that the object was cone-shaped and small—not more than about fifteen feet high and ten feet wide. Hopkins scheduled more hypnotic sessions to explore Linda's numbness and her inability to remember what happened after it started. Their appointment schedule was interrupted when Linda called Hopkins on November 30, 1989, distraught by what she remembered from the night before.

Linda went to bed late, long after her husband was asleep (he worked an early shift). As she got into bed at 3:15 a.m., the familiar numbness began. She tried and failed to wake up her husband. She saw something hiding behind the window drapes. The drapes parted, and a short, gray creature approached the bed. She threw a pillow at it and suddenly felt that she had done something terribly wrong. She had a fragmentary memory of a piece of white gauze floating in front of her face, and of sitting on a table while someone thumped lightly up and down her back. That was all she could consciously remember. This memory frightened and depressed her because she thought her unusual and upsetting experiences were behind her.

Under hypnosis, Linda recalled that several creatures had approached her and carried her paralyzed body toward her bedroom window. She was levitated through the metal child guard on the inside of the window and through the closed window into a beam of light outside. She hovered upright in this beam as her nightgown rose up around her face. A UFO was waiting just above her window, and she was floated up the light beam into the UFO.

Linda remembered seeing benches and instruments arranged along the walls of the UFO. Frightened and angry, she was led into a large room with an examination table. The occupants wanted her to get onto the table, and although she resisted they physically forced her onto it. She shouted angrily at them using sounds she did not understand. They examined her spine by thumping along her vertebrae. Then they examined inside her nose with various instruments. They examined her fingers, her toes, and her hair. They let her dress, walked her to a door, and then she remembered being back in bed, trying and failing to wake her husband.

• • •

At about 3:00 a.m. on the morning of November 30, a VIP security convoy drove south from midtown Manhattan along the East River on the FDR Drive. The convoy turned onto South Street, where the drive becomes an elevated highway. (Security convoys avoid elevated highways because they might be trapped and ambushed.) The convoy was heading to Battery Park, on the southern tip of Manhattan, to meet a ferry that would carry their VIP to a heliport on Governors Island. US security agent Dan, driving, was accompanied by agent Richard in the passenger seat. Their VIP was in the backseat. For no apparent reason the motors in the convoy cut out, and the convoy came to a stop on South Street near the Brooklyn Bridge and about five hundred feet from Linda's apartment building. Dan and Richard tried to radio agents in other cars, but the radio did not work. They asked the VIP to lie down in the backseat: the VIP took the unexpected turn of events good-humoredly and complied. The agents decided to do nothing for a few minutes and see if the sudden motor and radio failure would correct itself before taking the potentially risky step of leaving the car to get help.

Richard reached into his pocket for a stick of gum, and as he unwrapped it an orange glow reflected off the foil wrapper. He looked up to see what was making the glow and saw a reddish-orange UFO hovering over a nearby apartment building. Richard, Dan, and the VIP saw the UFO move away from the top of the building and then down the side until it was just above an apartment window. A beam of light shone down from the UFO. A small creature floated out of the apartment window into the beam. The creature was followed out the window by a woman dressed in a white nightgown that floated up over her head. Two other creatures followed the woman out of the window. They all remained suspended briefly in the light beam before floating up into the bottom of the UFO. The light beam disappeared, and the UFO flew over the Brooklyn Bridge to the south. They watched as it plunged into the East River just a few hundred yards beyond the bridge.

Dan and Richard had also read *Intruders*. They wrote to Hopkins, describing what they saw. Their letter, as Hopkins put it, "drove a spike straight through the heart of reason."[66] They had seen Linda Cortile's abduction.

• • •

On the same night, Janet Kimball (not her real name) was returning from Brooklyn to upstate New York. At about 3:00 a.m. she was halfway across the Brooklyn Bridge when her car lights dimmed and her motor cut out, as did the lights and motors of the other cars on the bridge. She looked to her right and saw a UFO hovering near an apartment building close to the bridge. She saw a small creature

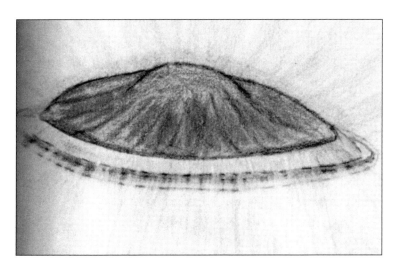

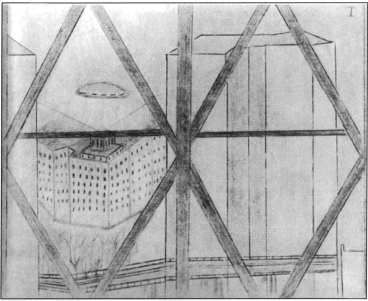

Figure 16. Drawings of the UFO that abducted Linda Cortile from her apartment in lower Manhattan in November 1989. Top drawing by Agent Richard; bottom drawing by Janet Kimball.

suspended above an apartment window, a woman below the creature, and two creatures below the woman. She saw them rise into the bottom of the UFO and saw the UFO fly directly over the bridge, where it disappeared from view behind the bridge's elevated walkway. Kimball saw the same thing Dan and Richard had seen.

Months later, Hopkins received a thick envelope containing Janet Kimball's drawings of her experience. The drawings were like Richard's drawing illustrating what he had seen of Linda Cortile's levitation into the UFO (see figure 16).

Hopkins also received an unsolicited letter from the VIP Richard and Dan were protecting (which I have seen). In it, the VIP acknowledged that he had shared the experience with Richard and Dan, whom he knew had been in contact with Hopkins. He apologized for not having contacted Hopkins sooner, marveled about the significance of the experience, and hoped that both he and Hopkins would enjoy reminiscing about it in their old age: "Won't it be amusing to sit back and watch all the nations of the world pull together. It shan't be long before the earth becomes whole again."[67] But the diplomat refused to publicly discuss his involvement with the experience, and signed the letter "The Third and Last Man." But Hopkins knew who the VIP was, and so will everyone else who knows anything about international politics and who reads *Witnessed*.

I met Linda Cortile while visiting Hopkins in 1992, before *Witnessed* was published. I sat through the hypnosis session described in that book.[68] Linda was resting on a couch, Hopkins was sitting in a chair to the right and behind her head, and I was sitting seven or eight feet away beyond Linda's feet. Hopkins began to induce hypnosis and I began to doze. Hopkins asked Linda to remember what happened in her bedroom on a night shortly after the November 30, 1989 abduction experience. She said she decided to check out something suspicions at the bedroom window curtains: "I just get up from bed and I walk to the window . . . *ooohhhhh!*" (bloodcurdling scream). That high-decibel scream snapped me out of my doze and

UFOs, ETs, and Alien Abductions

made me appreciate the emotional impact of a remembered abduction experience.

More than ten years after *Witnessed* was published, Budd Hopkins has died, Linda Cortile is still Linda Cortile, and the Third Man has taken the retirement he deserves. The complicated saga of security agents Dan and Richard has played out behind the closed doors of the US government, and I know nothing about it.

7

The Abduction Narrative

The Barney and Betty Hill case described in chapter 5 and the touchstone cases described in chapter 6 were presented there in detail. In this chapter the similarities among the six cases are reviewed and a common abduction narrative is constructed by drawing on evidence from each of those cases as well as from other cases reported to abduction researchers.

Abduction experiences can only be understood and evaluated by considering what is known about human memory and the circumstances that influence it. Those circumstances include individual differences in personality as well as the effect on memory of hypnosis and emotional trauma. Each of those influences is discussed in this chapter to support the conclusion that reported abduction experiences are memories of real events.

Abduction and Reality

Each of the abduction cases begins with unaided recall of a close encounter. In the New York City case the close encounter and the abduction were seen by witnesses; in the Buff Ledge case the departing UFO was seen by witnesses; in the other cases the abductee or abductees experienced the close encounter and the abduction by themselves. Each case includes conscious recall of a close encounter and conscious awareness of missing time. Each abductee experienced emotional changes: they were awed by the close encounter, they were inexplicably tired or irritable, and they were upset by the missing time. In some of the cases there was unprompted conscious memory of interaction with occupants, either immediately after the event (Linda Cortile in Manhattan and Michael Lapp at Buff Ledge) or later (Denis McMahon in West Nyack). Some cases involved unprompted dreams related to the abduction experience (Betty Hill and Jim Weiner of the Allagash abductees). The abduction experience was then recalled more fully as a result of either the passage of time or by aided recall involving hypnosis.

What you have read in this book about the disc- and cigar-shaped UFOs seen in the '50s or the low, big, and slow UFOs seen from the '80s onward is more or less the complete story of each case. But each of the six abduction cases is more complicated than the narrative summary presented here. My accounts emphasized the touchstone commonalities rather than the details that fill out the narrative, so it will be useful here to go beyond the outlines of the six cases and consider a broader summary of more cases in greater detail.

The Prototypical Abduction

Abduction researcher Thomas E. Bullard asked thirty-one other abduction researchers to complete and return a ninety-two-item questionnaire about themselves and the people they studied. Thirteen researchers responded. Bullard analyzed the data sent in by his thirteen respondents and collated the new data with eight previously published scholarly summaries of abduction accounts, including an earlier very large summary of his own.[69] He found that the accounts were consistent across researchers. While some researchers thought extraterrestrial contact was good for people and others did not, researcher attitude had little effect on the content of the abduction narrative.

A prototypical abduction report begins with a remembered close encounter. The next conscious memory occurs sometime after the close encounter. The reporter realizes that he or she cannot account for the time between the close encounter and the next remembered event, which may be driving along a road without remembering how he or she got there. The presence of occupants may be fleetingly remembered, but other than that the abductee may later recall only the anomalies: missing time, damaged clothing, nosebleeds, or feeling tired or irritable. Sometimes more than one person is abducted, but often other people with the abductee, if awake, are "turned off" and are not abducted, or if they are asleep, do not wake up.

The abduction narrative often begins with someone being removed from a car, but the abduction may also occur in an outdoor place or a bedroom at night.[70] More women report being abducted than men. There may be generalized anxiety or upset about the remembered close encounter, upsetting dreams involving an abduction experience, unexplained scars on the body, or unexplainable fears of a particular place or action.

Sometimes memory of what followed the close encounter is regained spontaneously. Sometimes the person who remembers the close encounter seeks help from a therapist or a UFO investigator because of generalized anxiety following the remembered experience, or because of upsetting dreams. Further details of an abduction experience may then emerge through relaxation therapy or regressive hypnosis that explores the period of missing time.

The abduction event begins when the abductee is moved away from the car, outdoor place, or bedroom, often by two or more occupants. The abductee sometimes passes through metal, glass, or wooden barriers, and may be levitated into a hovering UFO or walked or floated to a UFO resting on the ground. The abductee usually enters a disk-shaped craft with the occupants, who put him in a corridor or "waiting room" with other occupants and sometimes with other abductees. The occupants communicate words or feelings telepathically. The abductee is told or convinced to cooperate, feel reassured, and feel that things will return to normal after the occupants have carried out some simple tests.

The occupants described in a typical report are four-and-one-half to five-feet tall humanoids with a large head, large slanted black eyes, vestigial noses and ears, a slit for a mouth, and a face that tapers to a small pointed chin. Their arms, necks, and legs are thin but strong. Their hands have four long fingers. They wear a skin-tight garment that is usually gray like their skin, and their skin and fingers, when felt by an abductee, are cool and smooth. There is no noticeable sexual differentiation, but abductees sometimes report that behavior or expression may differentiate more feminine from more masculine occupants. Their clothes are usually featureless but some abductees report clothes with symbols or an insignia. Other types of reported occupants include a tall insect-like creature acting in the role of examiner, and occupants whose facial features are a blend of a terrestrial reptile and conventional humanoid and whose skin is rough and greenish. Occupants who are closer to human height and have human-like hair and facial features have also been reported. Sometimes shorter two-and-one-half to three-feet tall, gray-skinned humanoids are reported in the company of taller occupants.

A physical examination is the most common feature of an abduction experience. The abductee is led to and told to mount an examination table that rises as a block from the floor or is supported on a single pedestal. An occupant feels the abductee's vertebrae, moves the abductee's arms and legs, and investigates the abductee's hair, mouth, fingers, and toes. Surface skin samples may be taken with a scraper and stored. Metal probes with wires attached will be placed at various parts of the body while readouts may be visible on nearby screens. Sometimes a large eye-like machine is placed over the abductee and it scans from head to toe. Sampling is concentrated on the reproductive system. Men report being made to have an erection and semen is extracted and stored. Women report vaginal probes. Some abductees report that implants were placed in their nasal passages or deep inside an eye socket; others report that implants were removed from those locations.

After the examination, the occupants telepathically offer reassurance, provide a rationale for their activities, and offer hints about their origin and the historical continuity of their interaction with humans. The occupants sometime stage theatrics that the abductee either experiences telepathically or as external sounds and images. The theatrics are often catastrophe-oriented, showing images of Earth destroyed by astronomical forces, war, or an environmental disaster.

Some abducted women (rarely men) may be taken to a nursery where they are asked to physically and psychologically nurture small, pale children with wispy hair who are said to be their own hybrid offspring. They may also be shown incubators that appear to contain fetuses being nurtured in bottles. (Aldous Huxley imagined similar incubators in *Brave New World*, his dystopian novel published in 1932.)

Some abductees experience what are apparently journeys to either a larger vehicle farther from the Earth (as in the Buff Ledge encounter), or another physical environment which may or may not look like Earth. The abductee is not sure whether the physical environment is real, or, like the theatrics, simply staged.

Abductees are then returned from the disc-like abduction vehicle to where they were taken, often with no understanding of how they got back. The elapsed time is usually between one and two hours. The consciously recalled aftereffects of an abduction include the close encounter, the experience of missing time, flashbacks, dreams, and emotional reactions like those described in the six cases. The abductee may also discover new scars that cannot be accounted for. The typical scar is a short incision on the shin or calf or a semicircular scoop out of a knee or thigh. Some people report increased paranormal abilities following an abduction.

Two kinds of continuity are associated with abductions. An abductee may experience multiple abductions starting in young adolescence and continuing into early middle age, and abductions may be familial and generational, with parents and children being abducted in succession or together over many years.

Abduction Skeptics

The abduction skeptic thinks an abduction report is created by a disturbed personality interacting with an enabling researcher, with the result being a narrative that satisfies the needs of both the reporter and the researcher. The skeptic thinks abduction reporters have trouble distinguishing between fantasy and reality, and they believe their fantastic dreams or imaginings are true. The alleged abductees may be clinically normal, but they have "fantasy-prone personalities" or "weak boundaries" between fantasy and reality. The skeptic thinks that these people seek out untrained abduction researchers who do not recognize that the purported abductee cannot separate fantasy from reality. If the researcher uses hypnosis with an alleged abductee, all that results is a more complicated fantasy. The skeptic argues that abduction reports are false memories.

Abduction Psychology

People can certainly be persuaded to believe things that never happened.[71] Justice would be swift and fair, and history books would never disagree if the truth about past events was always clear. But justice is not always swift and fair, historians often disagree, and the truth can be elusive. Not all memory is false memory; establishing the truth about recalled abductions is a challenge many UFO and abduction researchers have successfully met.

I have met several of the abductees and investigators whose experiences and reports formed the basis of the six cases reviewed here, and I am familiar with all of the other abductees through colleagues who know them. My judgment and that of my colleagues is that there is no reason to doubt the competence or veracity of the abductees or the reporters, and the information presented about those six cases is credible. But opinion is not enough. Abduction researchers ask the same questions that skeptics ask: what kind of people report abductions? Because this is an after the fact question, any possible answer could mean several different things. If abduction reporters turn out to be like everybody else, it could mean *(a)* there was nothing special about them that led to the abduction experience, and the experience did nothing to change them or *(b)* the experience turned people who were abnormal before the abduction into normal people afterward. If abduction reporters are different from normal people, it could mean *(a)* only certain kinds of people experience an abduction, because, as skeptics argue, certain personality types are prone to report imaginary experiences; *(b)* only certain personality types are chosen to be abducted; or *(c)* the abduction experience turns normal people before the abduction into abnormal people afterward.

Personality and Memory

A group of abduction researchers, with the cooperation of two psychologists, studied nine abductees without resolving the logical conundrum outlined above. A PhD clinical psychologist who knew the common background of the nine abduction reporters found another PhD clinical psychologist who did not know their common background. The first psychologist asked the second psychologist to give each abduction reporter a regular, fee-paid psychological assessment which included an interview and a battery of psychological tests. The examining psychologist was told that the research group was studying creativity and was interested in similarities and differences among the study participants. The nine abduction reporters agreed not to mention their abduction experiences to the examining psychologist. The examining psychologist then interviewed and tested each abduction reporter and wrote a separate report about each person following the interview and testing. Then she wrote a final report that compared and contrasted the "Nine Psychologicals." Finally, a third PhD clinical psychologist who also did not know the abduction reporters' common experiences was paid to review and comment on five of the examining psychologist's nine interview reports. After the examining psychologist had completed her reports, the research sponsors told her about the common experiences of her nine clients. "She was, it is safe to say, flabbergasted," they wrote.

The psychologist then wrote a supplemental report based on that knowledge. The investigation was completed in 1983, and the final report was issued in 1985 by the nonprofit UFO research foundation that sponsored it.[72]

The Nine Psychologicals were all above average in intelligence and one was in the top range on the intelligence test. They were all college-educated, and two had graduate degrees. Their ages ranged from twenty-eight to forty-three when the examinations took place. They worked at white-collar occupations including secretary, audio technician, business executive, and corporate lawyer. Five were men and four were women. Four were unmarried, one was married, and four were divorced. Four reported serial abductions and several others were thought to have had serial abductions. Abductions were reported from as early as five or seven years old, and abductions were reported until as recently as three years before the study was started.

Examining psychologist Dr. Elizabeth Slater based her analysis on responses to the Wechsler Adult Intelligence Scale (WAIS), the Rorschach test, the Thematic Apperception Test (TAT), the Minnesota Multiphasic Personality Inventory (MMPI), and personal interviews. The outward personalities of the nine people ranged from exhibitionistic and dramatic to shy and reserved, and their predominant skills and abilities ranged from verbal to practical and mechanical. Despite these overt differences, their underlying emotional makeup was similar.

After having been told that they all had reported abductions, Dr. Slater wrote this comment in her supplemental report.

> The first and most critical question is whether our subjects'
> reported experiences could be accounted for strictly on the
> basis of psychopathology, i.e. mental disorder. The answer is
> a firm no.

She wrote that her subjects were not pathological liars, paranoid schizophrenics, or dissociative personalities, and nothing in their personality profiles suggested that they would either confabulate such experiences or lie about them. She did note that their anxiety, inner turmoil, weak sense of identity, and suspiciousness of others, while not proof (an after-the-fact correlation is never proof), were at least consistent with having experienced the powerlessness and trauma associated with the reported abduction experiences. The third psychologist who blind-reviewed five of Dr. Slater's seven individual reports and the summary report was satisfied that the diagnoses and descriptions in those reports were consistent with the interview notes and the psychological test results.

• • •

Another research group obtained mailing lists from fellow researchers of people who reported having been removed from normal terrestrial surroundings by non-human beings, taken to a spacecraft, and examined by and/or communicating telepathically or verbally with the occupants. The abduction reporters could have remembered these experiences consciously or recalled them through some memory-aiding technique like hypnosis, or a combination of both. Consciously recalled missing time was not a criterion, but people who just remembered strange creatures in the bedroom were excluded.[73]

Nineteen of these people completed the MMPI, the test used by Slater in her study of the Nine Psychologicals. They also completed tests to assess fantasy-proneness and hypnotic suggestibility. There was a questionnaire that recorded demographics, childhood experiences, sleep habits, and other factors that might relate to an abduction experience.

There was no difference between the abduction reporters and the general population (whose results were known from earlier studies) on the tests that assessed fantasy-proneness or hypnotic suggestibility. The MMPI produces a profile of scores for each person, and each score represents a different aspect of personality. The population results for each profile follow the well-known bell curve of human variation, and the score profile of each person who takes the MMPI can be compared to the population profile to see which scores lie within the "normal" range, and which scores are "outliers." The abduction reporters fell into both groups on the MMPI: normal and outlier, on several of the scales. The outlier group made responses that indicated more extreme feelings of depression and social and emotional alienation, lack of ego mastery, and bizarre sensory experiences. The people in the outlier group had personality characteristics like the nine abduction reporters studied by Elizabeth Slater, while the people in the first group were just like everybody else. The difference between the two groups on their MMPI profiles was not related to the abduction experiences they reported. In fact, some members who shared the same abduction experience tested into different groups.

• • •

Another more recent study involved people responding to invitations posted on UFO websites to contact researchers if they had experienced an abduction. The sample also included a few people reporting an abduction who had been interviewed earlier by abduction researchers. Twenty-six people in the group who claimed to have experienced an abduction were compared to twenty-six people who did not claim to have been abducted but who matched the group of abduction reporters in age and gender. Again, the main interest was test scores for fantasy-proneness, and again the people reporting abductions were no more fantasy-prone than the control group.[74] The abductees were in fact little different from the matched nonreporters in any of the tested aspects of their personality. (The MMPI was not used in this study.)

• • •

Although skeptics argue that abduction reports are made by fantasy-prone people, the research reported here shows that abduction reports are made by people who are no more and no less fantasy-prone than anyone else. The research also shows that some people who report abductions are outliers on the Minnesota Multiphasic Personality Inventory, but others are normal. This weakens the skeptic's argument that the reports derive from idiosyncratic personality charac-

UFOs, ETs, and Alien Abductions

teristics of the reporters. It is important to remember that after the fact personality characteristics of people who report abductions cannot prove or disprove the truth of an abduction report.

Hypnosis and Memory

Hypnosis and recovered memory are hot topics in contemporary psychology. Since hypnosis has been used with many abduction reporters, an explanation of how memory works and how hypnosis affects it is in order.

Consciousness and Memory

Modern psychologists agree with Sigmund Freud, the inventor of psychoanalysis, that we are influenced by mental activity of which we are unaware. The mental activity that produces language, memories, and emotions occurs without direction from our "verbal" selves; words come unbidden to the lips, memories spring unbidden to the mind, and emotions come unbidden to the heart. Freud theorized that strong emotions or unpleasant thoughts related to sex or aggression can be kept out of awareness by a psychologically costly mental activity called repression, which suppresses the undesired emotions and thoughts and then transforms the suppressed emotions and thoughts into less threatening but sometimes equally dysfunctional thoughts, feelings, or behavior.

Modern psychologists take the broader view that unconscious feelings and experiences are not just the result of sexual urges or anger. Nevertheless, therapists still often work more or less as Freud did, trying to make clients aware of their hidden thoughts and feelings that might be related to their unhappiness or dysfunctional behavior.

This is good news, but it is also bad news. The bad news is that a theory validating the existence of unconscious feelings and experiences empowers incompetent or politically-motivated therapists to persuade clients that their current unhappiness was caused by people who did unremembered bad things to them a long time ago. During the 1980s controversies arose in the United States about the so-called "recovered memories" of women whose therapists suggested that their unhappiness stemmed from a history of repressed childhood sexual abuse. Families were broken and fathers sent to jail on the testimony of patients whose "recovered memories" included scenes of parental sexual abuse that had been coached into them by therapists.[75] In some cases it was finally proven that the sexual abuse never happened, and the entire episode was a construction of the therapist's imagination transferred to the mind of a client as if it had been fact.

The good news is that there is clear evidence that memories of trauma and stress can be repressed and these memories can later be recalled using a variety of methods, including the externally focused attention to personal experience that is hypnosis.

Hypnosis

Hypnosis can be used both to suppress memories and then, later on, to recall them. When therapeutic hypnosis reestablishes memories of trauma and stress, the result is often the emotional catharsis that was the goal of Freudian analysis and its modern successors. Freud in fact started his pioneering work on neuroses by using hypnosis.

Hypnosis withdraws attention from most of the senses and concentrates it on a limited sensory input, usually the hypnotist's voice. Responding to instructions from the hypnotist, the subject is directed to attend to internal feelings, images, and remembered experiences. The therapist may encourage the hypnotized client to reexperience past events, and the recall may help a client to reexperience and then overcome emotional conflicts based on those events.[76]

Not all people are hypnotizable, and among those who are there are differences in the degree to which their "state of mind" changes under hypnosis. Some people respond to suggestions about their muscles and movements; some respond to suggestions about what

UFOs, ETs, and Alien Abductions

they should or should not be thinking about; and some can be made to lose almost all sensory contact with the external world, with the result being that the hypnotist's suggestions may produce profound changes in their perceptions, thoughts, and actions.

Hypnosis changes both conscious experience and its accompanying brain state. Some highly hypnotizable people do not feel pain following a pinprick, extreme cold, extreme heat, a knife cut, dental surgery, or abdominal surgery.[77] Changes in brain wave activity and blood flow in the brain accompany the hypnotic reduction of experienced pain.[78]

Hypnosis does not improve memory accuracy. With or without hypnosis, what is retained and remembered after an event may not be what actually happened, and an originally imperfect memory can be further changed by words or experiences long after the event.[79] But any form of guided repetition, in particular the relaxed and mentally concentrated state known as hypnosis, can help people to retrieve previously stored memories (accurate or inaccurate) that for one reason or another are not currently available to conscious experience.[80]

Traumatic Amnesia

The abduction narratives described earlier included periods of amnesia ("missing time") following a consciously recalled UFO close encounter. Hypnosis is commonly used to overcome amnesia. Although we may think that we deal with the world around us through reasoning and memory, our muscles, bones, glands, internal organs, and circulatory and respiratory systems beg to differ. Trauma can have as permanent an effect on our brain and body as it does on our conscious mind (and the parts of the brain that allow us to think and remember). When you are in a dangerous situation, anxiety, fear, and anger act on the body, changing heart rate, respiratory rate, muscle tension, and blood pressure, and triggering the production of hormones that prepare the body for "fight or flight."[81] After the fearsome event is over, you may never want to remember it again—and sometimes you may never remember, but this comes at a price.

Following in the footsteps of Freud and other early researchers, the psychiatric profession now calls the situation when the bodily changes associated with fear or anxiety persist without the memory of the precipitating event, "dissociative disorder." In other words, if a similar situation were to occur, your body, based on your past experience, would react by preparing for fight or flight, but you would not know why. Imagine that you suffer a wounding snub at a dinner party. Your mental and physical reaction at the time was shame and humiliation, which are milder surrogates for fear and anger. The next time you are invited to a dinner party, anticipating the same experience produces the bodily reactions and feelings based on your last bad experience, but you do not know why—because your emotionally upsetting memory of the event has been repressed out of consciousness. You experience free-floating anxiety whenever you anticipate any event bearing a resemblance to a dinner party: a gathering of friends, an outdoor picnic, or a group of strangers. Feeling anxious in many situations, and not knowing why, is one reason people go to therapists.

Some therapists will try to calm the pounding heart and eliminate the anxious discomfort without knowing what caused them—and of course you can't tell the therapist, because you can't remember. The therapist puts you into as calm and relaxed a situation as possible and has you imagine going to a dinner party or other social event. If this exercise is done competently, eventually you will associate some of that calm relaxation with the imagined experience, and your fight or flight emotional reaction will be reduced.

But the memory associated with the original upset is still there, and unless it can be brought to consciousness and discussed and treated the same way, it still has the capacity to precipitate fight or flight reactions when least expected. That missing memory may appear as a dream, it may recur spontaneously, or a therapist may help it to emerge into consciousness by relaxing the patient and providing a secure and nonthreatening environment in which to talk about anxiety-producing situations.

One way to produce a secure, nonthreatening environment is to induce hypnosis in an appropriately hypnotizable patient. Once the memory has been recalled under hypnosis, the emotional effects of the conscious memory itself can be treated in a variety of ways. When the symptoms have been reduced and the power of the memory to elicit new symptoms has been eliminated, the therapist's work is done and the patient is cured. Amnesia can and does follow traumatic events, and when the amnesia is removed, either through spontaneous flashbacks, dreams, or hypnotic induction, symptoms of distress can be relieved.[82]

The abduction cases described earlier began with the conscious memory of a close encounter, followed by a period of amnesia, and then free-floating symptoms of emotional distress. Conscious memory of the abduction was regained through some combination of spontaneous recall, dreams, flashbacks, or hypnotic induction. The pattern of amnesia and anxiety occurring after a close encounter, followed by later retrieval of the even more distressing abduction memory, is consistent with the phenomenon of memory dissociation following a traumatic event.

Hypnotically Induced Amnesia

It is possible to "postdate" suggestions during hypnosis so that they take effect after the patient has returned to normal consciousness. Hypnotized people can be told to "forget" life experiences they have just discussed and to forget the entire hypnosis session, creating "missing time" after the trance is ended. These suggestions can be post-hypnotically canceled by an instruction issued during the trance state. For example, during a hypnotic trance, the hypnotist might say, "Forget what you just told me about your first day at university after you have come out of the trance until I say 'Now you can remember everything.'"[83] The trance is ended, the hypnotist asks for a description of the subject's first day at university, and the subject cannot remember.

The hypnotist says "Now you can remember everything" and the subject remembers the first day at university. Hypnotic suggestion to forget (as used by Dr. Benjamin Simon with Barney and Betty Hill) prevents conscious post-hypnotic recall and has measurable effects on brain electrical activity.[84] Hypnotic suggestion can help to make previously repressed memories accessible to consciousness, but it can also turn consciously available memories into at least temporarily repressed ones.

Abductees who are hypnotized to recover memories of what happened during their "missing time" often report that they feel anxiety and foreboding as they attempt to recall what happened.[85] If, as abductees report, they experience something like an altered state of consciousness (hypnosis) while being abducted, and if, as abductees report, their abductors say they should not remember what happened, then the therapist who hypnotizes an abductee may be working against the occupants' post-hypnotic suggestion to forget what happened during the abduction. *That suggestion was never post-hypnotically canceled!* Not only may an abduction memory be traumatic, but it may also have been preconditioned *not* to be remembered, making it even harder to recall.

Hypnosis, Recovered Memory, and Abduction Memories

Some, but not all, of the remembered abduction details obtained from the fourteen people in the six cases summarized earlier were obtained under hypnosis. All of those cases involved:

• Witnesses who experienced a UFO close encounter

• The conscious experience of missing time

• Emotional distress about the experiences

• And, in many of the cases, observable and reportable physical and mental effects following the close encounter.

In the Barney and Betty Hill case, there were Betty's dreams, Barney's flashbacks, his warts, the malfunctioning compass and watches, the recovered earrings, and the marks on the car. In the Buff Ledge incident, there were independent witnesses to the close encounter and the emotional state of the abductees following the event. In the West Nyack, New York case there were flashbacks and the missing time recorded on the police blotter. Jim Weiner of the Allagash Four had dreams, and all four of them had reportable emotional consequences. The Kansas abductees suffered irritated eyes as well as emotional aftereffects. Linda Cortile's spectacular New York abduction near the Brooklyn Bridge started with her conscious memory of occupants. The close encounter, the occupants, and her abduction were witnessed independently by at least four people. The hypnosis accounts are largely consistent across the six cases described here, and across many others not described in detail but summarized in several sources.[86]

Human memory is a clumsy tool for learning what happened in the past because memory is "reconstituted" every time it is evoked, and every time it is reconstituted it can be modified by suggestions made from other people or even by oneself (the "one that got away" gets bigger and bigger with each retelling).[87] Since memory is reconstitutable and modifiable, it cannot by itself be trusted to define the reality of a past event. A more valid understanding of the past is gained from multiple witnesses, because each witness's memory may have been influenced differently between the event in question and the present. Consistencies among witnesses provide evidence about the core of what happened; the inconsistencies may be the result of variations during the reconstitution. This was why the British scientific intelligence officer R. V. Jones needed touchstones of facts that had been corroborated several times to justify his confidence in information provided by informants about German rocket development during World War II.

If memory is a difficult tool for reconstructing the past, then the relaxed and withdrawn state of mind called hypnosis, during which the hypnotized person's mental activity can be at least partly directed by the hypnotist, is an even more difficult, albeit powerful, tool. Hypnosis can have a dramatic effect on the availability of memory; it can facilitate or inhibit memory, but it cannot improve it. Fear, anxiety, and previous hypnotic instruction can all prevent memories that have already been encoded and stored from being made available to conscious experience. Hypnotically delivered instructions can block conscious memory either of particular previous events or of an entire hypnosis session itself. On the other hand, hypnosis is widely used in therapy to overcome the repression or dissociation that prevents memories of past traumatic events from being consciously experienced. But it is important to remember that imaginary events can be described by others so convincingly that people can sometimes be made to mistakenly accept them as part of their own personal experience.

The Intelligence Analysis

The facts are that some people report unusual and upsetting experiences following close encounters with UFOs. Many of them report missing time immediately following the encounter, and emotional and physical aftereffects often follow. Occasionally, an abduction experience is recalled through a memory flashback or a dream, often soon after the close encounter experience, but sometimes months or years later. More often, the person who remembers the close encounter and the missing time, and who has experienced physical symptoms or emotional upset, seeks help to relieve the distress and understand the experience.

The best-known abduction experiences are the ones that have been investigated by therapists and researchers who take those reports seriously. Some of these helpers—a mixed group of qualified professionals and serious amateurs—use hypnosis to help the abductee overcome the amnesia that follows the close encounter. When hypnosis successfully recovers a remembered abduction experience, it is usually consistent with the experiences reported by other abductees at other times and places.

Abduction reporters themselves are not abnormally fantasy-prone, as we have established; nor are they more susceptible to being hypnotized than the average person. Some, but not all of them, deviate from the norm on certain personality characteristics—being more suspicious, less trusting, and having a weaker sense of personal identity than the average—but there is no *a priori* reason, as psychologist Elizabeth Slater made clear, to suspect that the average abduction reporter is more likely than the average person to lie about an abduction experience or fail to distinguish between a fantasy and reality. Either the reported abduction experience is more or less correct evidence about something that did actually happen (taking into account that even the best memory is less than perfect), or it is an unwitting fabrication produced as a collaborative effort by the reporter and the researcher/helper.

Are Abduction Reports True?

If abduction reports are fabrications, then they are consistent fabrications across many cases. Consistent fabrications might be caused by the abduction reporter having absorbed a generic abduction report from our cultural milieu and adapted it to fit a particular time and place, or they might be caused by an abduction researcher/helper "feeding" the purported abductee that same generic report, which is then adapted by the purported abductee to a particular time and place.

But this theory does not explain the original close encounter and missing time that occur in every reliable case: those experiences did not arise from aided memory—they were consciously recalled. The fabrication theory also doesn't explain the consciously remembered and reported flashbacks and dreams that are consistent with the hypnotically aided reports and would, in other circumstances, be consistent with a diagnosis of traumatic dissociative amnesia. Finally, the fabrication theory is not consistent with the investigation protocols of skilled abduction researchers who use hypnosis to overcome traumatic or hypnotic amnesia and who know how to avoid the danger of generating hypnotic fantasies by asking leading questions.[88]

You have to decide between two alternatives. First, that hypnosis has been used to overcome traumatic amnesia and/or post-hypnotic amnesia—two things hypnosis can do. Second, that hypnosis has been used to produce a false "recovered memory" of something that did not happen—something else hypnosis can do. The memories that emerge under hypnosis are consistent with memories that arise through flashbacks, unaided direct recall, and dreams. Both the hypnotically recovered memories and the other memories are evidence about what happened during a consciously remembered period of "missing time" following a UFO close encounter.

Based on the consistency of the evidence, its congruence with other aspects of the experience, and its congruence with non-hypnotically obtained evidence, I think that hypnotically recovered abduction memories following a close encounter and missing time are accurate (within the limits of memory accuracy) accounts of what happened during the period of missing time. I think that the six cases described earlier, as well as many others, show that extraterrestrial occupants have abducted people into UFOs, examined them, interacted with them in other ways, and then, after one to two hours, returned them to Earth.

PART THREE

Us

When a distinguished but elderly scientist states that something is possible, he is almost certainly right. When he states that something is impossible, he is very probably wrong.

—Sir Arthur Clarke

8

What We Know

Twenty-first century media document the adventures of anthropologists, archaeologists, geologists, and naturalists who study every culture, geographical anomaly, and ecological niche on our planet. But one adventure excluded from this lively quest for knowledge is our study of the creatures who are studying us.[89] Science and the media largely ignore our own efforts to understand the extraterrestrial exploration of our planet and the extraterrestrials' study of ourselves. The next chapters of this book aim to correct that omission. This chapter summarizes what we know about UFOs; chapter 9 explains why science and the media ignore UFOs; and chapter 10, which outlines the recent history of our social and political response to UFOs, concludes by proposing how we should deal with UFOs, ETs, and alien abductions.

A Summary of the Evidence

The modern North American UFO chronology begins in 1947, but UFOs were seen in America and elsewhere during and immediately after the Second World War—and there is suggestive evidence from the nineteenth century and long before. The modern evidence consists of photographs, landing traces, radar plots, and eyewitness testimony, often from civilian and military pilots, policemen, and other experienced observers.

UFOs are observed worldwide. There is no way to estimate the effect of vagaries of reporting (media interest and availability, government policy, witness reliability, public opinion) on the tally of the times and places where UFOs turn up, but there have been irregular temporal cycles in the frequency of reports, at least in the Western world, for the past fifty years or so.

Some UFOs that have been observed close up are hot enough to burn skin when touched. They also emit short-wave electromagnetic radiation that produces radiation poisoning at close range. The electromagnetic radiation ionizes the air around the UFO, causing a luminous halo at night and sometimes a blurry or shimmering halo in daylight.

UFOs range from very small (a few feet in diameter) to gigantic (miles in length or diameter). Their shapes include the classic two saucers face-to-face, Saturn-shaped discs, small eggs or spheres, large cigar-shaped craft, and giant triangular, rectangular, spherical, or boomerang-shaped objects that move very slowly at very low altitudes and then disappear rapidly. The performance of all of these machines exceeds that of the most advanced terrestrial aircraft.

UFOs can disable the weapons systems of military aircraft and land-based intercontinental ballistic missiles (ICBMs).

Many UFOs have crews. Sometimes small flying saucers have a visible crew of two occupants in a transparent dome. Larger UFOs are reported to have larger crews. The occupants have humanoid features (a head, two arms, two legs) in a variety of complexions, heights, and widths. Some occupants are small, perhaps two or three feet tall, and are seen wearing what appears to be the occupant equivalent of a spacesuit. The common variety of occupant, seen in or near UFOs by abductees, is a gray (either skin or clothing, or both) humanoid between four and five feet tall with skinny limbs, a thin neck, a large cranium tapering to a face with narrow chin, a thin line of a mouth, vestigial nostrils and ear openings, four fingers, and, most noticeably, large, oval black eyes that slope upward and outward.

People driving at night on deserted roads have been paced by low-flying UFOs. Their cars may be stopped or they may be enticed by curiosity or telepathic suggestion out of their cars and into the power of the occupants, who communicate telepathically with the abductees and take them into UFOs. Abductees are sometimes walked or dragged into a landed UFO, but they can also be levitated upward inside a beam of light into a hovering UFO. During an abduction, occupants may conduct tests on abductees, and an implant may be inserted into the nose or under an eye; conversely, sometimes an implant is removed. The occupants also convey apocalyptic or warning messages about the future of Earth. They also sometimes show abductees what appear to be hybrid occupant-human children. Abductees are generally returned to the same location from which they were abducted, with strong suggestions not to remember the abduction experience. The suggestion to forget sometimes fails outright, is short-circuited by dreams or flashbacks, or is removed using some form of assisted recall including but not limited to hypnosis.

People may be abducted from isolated locations in or near camps or cabins, or from their homes or apartments, and they experience more or less the same sequence of events. The experience is psychologically disturbing even when it is not consciously remembered, but it does not appear to produce serious permanent physical injury.

The *modus operandi* of UFO occupants is familiar because we treat animals just like UFO occupants treat us. Consider bears. We fly over their habitat in helicopters. We shoot a tranquilizing dart into a bear and when it is unconscious we land, haul it away in a net, and carry out tests either in a lab or on the spot. Then we put a telemetry chip under the bear's skin so we can track where it goes, and we return it to the general area where we found it, after which the bear wakes up and goes about its life. We can't interview bears, so we have no idea how they recall the experience. But the experience that we impose on some bears is not unlike the experience UFO occupants impose on some of us.

How UFOs Might Work

While I was a faculty associate of the Pulp and Paper Research Institute, the applied science and engineering laboratory of Canada's pulp and paper industry, I learned that engineers are more interested in UFOs than are scientists. Engineers are professional builders, so if someone tells an engineer about a new machine he or she will want to know how it works. Scientists are professional explainers. If someone tells a scientist about a new machine, but it cannot be understood using existing scientific theory, there is nothing scientific for the scientist to explain and so nothing to think about professionally. In the introduction I described the neuroscientist who saw a UFO while driving on the Taconic State Parkway—and ignored it.

Unconventional Flying Objects

Aeronautical engineer Paul R. Hill worked from 1939 to 1970 for the National Advisory Committee for Aeronautics (NACA), the US government agency that designed airplanes, bombs, and rockets during the Second World War. (In 1958 NACA became NASA—the National Aeronautics and Space Administration.) Hill designed the fuselage of the World War II P-47 fighter-bomber.

On July 16, 1952, during the Washington, DC "UFO flap," Hill saw some new machines. UFOs flew over NACA's Hampton Roads, Virginia headquarters, about 150 miles south of Washington, DC. As a good engineer, Hill wanted to know how they worked. As a good observer, he learned a great deal about how they worked from watching them. As a good scholar, he learned even more by reading other people's reports. Hill wrote *Unconventional Flying Objects,* a brilliant and informative book about UFO technology, during the 1970s.[90] NASA policy prohibited him from publishing information or opinion about UFOs under his own name, so the book was only published in 1995, after his death.[91]

UFOs, ETs, and Alien Abductions

Hill's book is so well written and has so many examples that the argument is clear even if the reader cannot follow the mathematics. One of the book's great virtues is that Hill followed a rule laid down by that most respectable skeptic, R. V. Jones, about evaluating intelligence. In Hill's words,

> UFO data-pattern correlation is my way of separating UFO fact from UFO fiction . . .[92] New facts and theories have to form a neat, logical package before they can be accepted, and justifiably so; otherwise technological chaos would reign. Therein lies the problem. Some degree of technological sense has to be made of the unconventional object, even to make "seeing believing."[93]

Like Jones, Hill needed consistency in deciding whether or not to accept new information, with the goal being to build a coherent understanding of a new situation from fragmentary but reliable pieces of information. Hill found consistencies across many UFO accounts, and based on those he derived an explanation of UFO function that lacked only one important detail: he could not explain how UFOs generated the antigravity force field that he believed was necessary to explain their performance.

UFOs are heavy. Evidence from compressed soil and deformed railroad ties at UFO landing sites allowed Hill to estimate that a small UFO (twenty feet long by ten feet high) weighed about thirty tons. Based on estimates of UFO weight and volume, Hill calculated that UFOs, like submarines, have a density about that of water, which may explain why UFOs can dive into and emerge from bodies of water, as reported in the Buff Ledge and New York City abduction cases (see chapter 6).

Hill wrote that the parched soil and charred roots left behind by hovering or landed UFOs were caused by short-range microwave radiation in the X-ray to near gamma ray frequency range. The microwave radiation ionizes the air around the UFO, making the temporarily energized electrons emit visible photons (light) as they drop back to their un-energized state. The reddish-orange glow or halo that surrounds UFOs seen at night and the sometimes foggy or blurry outlines seen at close range during the day is visible evidence of ionization.

While driving along a back road on the Texas-Arkansas border in 1980, Betty Cash, Vickie Landrum, and Betty's grandson Colby all suffered skin burns and radiation poisoning when they had a close encounter with a UFO that blocked their path. Stefan Michalak approached and touched a landed UFO in Canada in 1967, and he suffered skin burns and radiation poisoning.[94]

As the UFO lifts off and speeds up, the ionized glow changes from red-orange to bluish-white, which is consistent with an increase of microwave energy. According to Hill, microwave radiation is a side effect of the propulsion system, which employs a focusable anti-gravity force field. This field is directed downward from the bottom of the UFO, so in order to maneuver, the UFO tilts and points the force field opposite to the desired direction of travel (see figure 17). Another smaller component of the force field pointed in the direction of travel acts as a energy buffer that prevents occupants from being torn apart by the UFO's high acceleration.

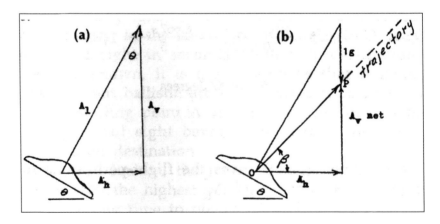

Figure 17. UFO propulsion dynamics as explained by aeronautical engineer Paul R. Hill.

UFOs, ETs, and Alien Abductions

UFOs do not emit any kind of chemical exhaust, nor do they emit charged particles. Hill argued that chemical exhaust would be detectible afterward and that charged particles would produce much higher radioactivity levels than those recorded at UFO landing sites. UFOs also do not emit photon beams (light particles) because, based on Hill's calculations, a photon beam powerful enough to lift a UFO would excavate a giant chasm and boil away the water in the Earth below the UFO. Hill reported UFO speeds based on radar data as upward of 9,000 miles per hour and accelerations in the range of 100 Gs (100 times the force of terrestrial gravity).

Although hot to the touch when landed, UFO surfaces in flight are not extremely hot: they emit a modest amount of infrared radiation. Hill proposed that a component of the antigravity force field projected in the direction of flight would absorb energy from compressed air ahead of the UFO and prevent the UFO from overheating.

Hill speculated that interstellar flights at speeds that (from a terrestrial reference point) approach the speed of light would be relatively short in time as measured on the UFO. For example, the trip to Alpha Centauri, a binary star system 4.37 light-years away, might be made from a standing start to a standing finish in just six weeks of time *elapsed on board*, assuming the ship reaches 0.9999 the velocity of light by accelerating at 140 Gs.

What UFOs and Occupants Can Do

Levitation

While Barney and Betty Hill walked or were dragged into a landed UFO, Michael Lapp and Susan Cornell were levitated off a dock into a hovering UFO inside a bright beam of light. The Allagash abductees were levitated out of their canoe into a hovering UFO inside a bright beam of light. Susan and Jennifer, the Kansas abductees, were levitated out of their car into a hovering UFO inside a bright beam of light. Security agents Richard and Dan watched Linda Cortile levitate through a closed window with a metal child guard and into a hovering UFO inside a bright beam of light.

Weapons System Interference:
The 1976 Tehran, Iran UFO Incident

In the fall of 1976, in the Shah's Iran, a UFO was seen and painted on radar over Tehran at an altitude of about 6,000 feet. The Air Force sent up an F-4 Phantom fighter jet to intercept it. As the jet approached, the UFO outran it and jammed its radios. When the jet abandoned the chase, the radios started to work again. A second Phantom took off, piloted by squadron commander Parviz Jafari. Jafari saw flashing red, green, orange, and blue lights ahead of him, but he could not see the object behind them. His backseat radar operator picked up the UFO at a distance of twenty-seven miles and they chased it at a closing speed of 150 knots. As they shortened the range Major Jafari thought about arming his missiles. Suddenly the UFO sped farther away and launched a round, bright object that headed straight toward the Phantom. Jafari armed a heat-seeking missile but as he tried to fire at the approaching object his weapons control panel and radio failed. He turned away from the oncoming object, which stopped short of a head-on collision. Jafari and his radar operator saw the object rejoin the UFO. Then a second object was ejected from the UFO, circled his fighter, and knocked out his communications and weapons systems again. When it moved away his radios worked again, he reported what had happened to his commander on the ground, and he was told to land.

The next day's debriefing session included a US Air Force officer. Jafari became a general in the Shah's Air Force and left the country after the Iranian Revolution in 1979. His account is included in Leslie Kean's book, *UFOs: Generals, Pilots, and Government Officials Go On the Record*, which describes other confrontations between military pilots and UFOs, some of which led to shooting at, but never shooting down, a UFO.

Malmstrom Air Force Base UFO/Missile Incident

In the 1960s, the US Air Force installed nuclear-armed Minuteman ICBMs in hardened silos dispersed over wide areas across the American west. Flights of ten missiles were controlled from an under-

UFOs, ETs, and Alien Abductions

ground bunker that communicated electronically with individual missile silos. Maintenance crews visited the missile silos regularly, and the entire missile field was patrolled by armed security guards. Being part of a missile launch crew required psychological stability, a high security clearance, and a tolerance for endless boring routine. It was also a good gig if you wanted to study while working, so an ambitious young officer could volunteer for the work and be assured of a quiet, climate-controlled environment with few distractions.

Second Lieutenant Robert Salas, USAF, studying for a master's degree in engineering, was on duty as the missile launch officer in the launch control bunker of Oscar Flight at Malmstrom Air Force Base in central Montana in the early hours of March 16, 1967. A security guard in the missile field called Salas to say that there were strange lights in the sky. After some discussion about what they might be, Salas told the guard to "just keep watching them and let me know if they get any closer," and went back to his books.

The guard called again: "Sir, there's one hovering outside the front gate."

"One what?"

"A UFO! It's just sitting there. We're all just looking at it. What do you want us to do?"

"What? What does it look like?"

"I can't really describe it. It's glowing red. What are we supposed to do?"

"Make sure the site is secure and I'll phone the command post."[95]

Moments later alarms went off in the launch control bunker. The flight of ten missiles had failed to no-go status—they could not be launched.[96] The missile's guidance and control system registered a fault. At or about the same time, ten missiles from nearby Echo Flight were also disabled, and security guards reported UFOs hovering over the Echo Flight silos. It took a full day to bring the Oscar Flight missiles back to ready status.

Post-incident follow-ups failed to find a power, electronic component, or software failure in the missiles or in the missile system. Missile manufacturer Boeing was able to duplicate the failure by introducing pulsed electronic "noise" into a component of the guidance and control system, but they could not explain how such a pulse got into the systems.[97] Internal documents corroborate the correlation between the time of UFO intrusions and the time of missile failure at Oscar and Echo Flights, although the Air Force denied the UFO rumor in its official history of the missile wing.

Occupant Telepathy

Engineers and physical scientists are not the only professionals who confront anomalous information from UFO and occupant encounters; psychologists also have to change some of their preconceptions in the face of new information. One preconception concerns extra-sensory perception (ESP). Despite a strong interest in ESP around the turn of the twentieth century[98] and a continuous low level of interest and publication ever since, ESP is not taken seriously within the field of scientific psychology, and ESP research is not supported by government funding agencies. This is for the same reason that physical scientists ignore UFO evidence: there is no physical theory explaining how it works. ESP may happen, but we have no idea how it happens, so it is not worth studying—at least not with government support.

Occupants communicate telepathically with abductees. They put words or commands into the minds of abductees at the start of an abduction, and they communicate telepathically during the abduction itself. Betty Hill said she heard her captor's words in an unfamiliar language but understood them as if they were in English.[99] Michael Lapp said he heard an occupant's voice "in his head" and that the occupant said "this is what you call telepathy."[100] Jim Weiner, one of the Allagash abductees, said communicating with the occupants was by "a strong telepathic impression":

Q: Did they say anything to you?

No, but I know that's what they want me to do, so I figured that I might as well do it.[101]

UFOs, ETs, and Alien Abductions

Jennifer and Susan, abducted in Kansas, also said the occupants communicated with them telepathically.[102] Linda Cortile in New York got reassuring mental messages from some of the occupants who abducted her:

I'm gonna go home now. That's what he's going to do. He must be able to read my mind . . .

Q: Do you use English? Regular English?

A: No. I'm thinking it. And he knows, and that's what he does.[103]

Extra-sensory perception is an inefficient means of communication at best when it can be demonstrated between human beings, but it is a normal and useful means of communication between humans and occupants.

What We Don't Know

Besides Paul R. Hill, no scientifically or technically trained writer has tried to systematically explain how UFOs work or what UFO occupants can do. Hill had the technical knowledge and the imagination to piece together the UFO observables and propose that UFOs modified gravity, but he didn't claim to know how they did that. No one has tried to explain how UFOs disable airborne weapons systems or ICBMs in missile silos. No psychological writer has tried to explain how UFO occupants communicate telepathically. And, as the next chapter will show, institutional science has shown no particular interest in trying to answer any of these questions.

9

Science and UFOs

S cience has had a hard time dealing with the evidence about UFOs. There are precedents for what should be done, but there are also disincentives against doing it. The precedents will be described first; the disincentives afterward.

Inductive Science

John Stuart Mill explained how to study the UFO and abduction evidence in his *System of Logic:*

> When, from the observation of a number of individual instances, we ascend to a general proposition, or when, by combining a number of general propositions, we conclude from them a proposition even more general, the process, which is substantially the same in both instances, is called Induction.[104]

Albert Einstein described the same starting point for all of science in *The Meaning of Relativity*:

> We are accustomed to regard as real those sense perceptions which are common to different individuals, and which therefore are, in a measure, impersonal. The natural sciences, and in particular the most fundamental of them, physics, deal with such sense perceptions. The conception of physical bodies, in

particular of rigid bodies, is a relatively constant complex of such sense perceptions.[105]

The philosopher of science Alfred North Whitehead wrote:

> A law of nature is merely an observed persistence of pattern in the observed succession of natural things: Law is then merely description. . . . The pre-occupation of science is then the search for simple statements which in their joint effect will express every thing of interest concerning the observed recurrences.[106]

J. Allen Hynek, the pioneer astronomer in the UFO field, spent a good part of his professional life sorting out the Unknowns from the Knowns and then putting the Unknowns into various UFO and occupant categories. Building on the work of Hynek and many other researchers, our scientific goal, in Whitehead's language, is to find "simple statements which in their joint effect will express everything of interest concerning the observed recurrences."[107] The observed recurrences are the UFO phenomena and the associated observations of UFO occupants and occupant behavior.

Those experiences that establish the reality of UFOs, occupants, and abductions are sometimes raw eyewitness accounts of phenomena but are equally often the outputs from instruments like cameras and radars. The ensemble of these consistent sense perceptions allow us to identify a class of Einstein's "physical bodies" that we call UFOs. The consistent multiple accounts of remembered experiences called abductions cannot be explained away as psychological abnormalities because the people who remember being abducted are not psychologically abnormal. This class of sense impression is consistent with other evidence about the existence of UFO occupants, and the witness accounts describe a consistent class of occupant behavior.[108]

From the performance of UFOs, and from the appearance, behavior, and physical and mental abilities demonstrated by the humanoids associated with them, I conclude that the machines were not made on our planet and their creators do not come from here.

That is why the simplest way to classify these phenomena is to call them observations of extraterrestrial vehicles, some of which have extraterrestrial crews.

The Psychology of Modern Science

Despite the preexisting advice about the importance of observational evidence and the overwhelming observational evidence available, the professional scientific community has ignored or ridiculed the study of UFOs and close encounters ever since routine observations made that study relevant more than fifty years ago. The work

Figure 18. Four scholars whose theories explain why scientists, mainstream media, and government officials ignore the UFO evidence. From upper left, proceeding clockwise: William James, Sigmund Freud, Thomas S. Kuhn, and Leon Festinger.

of two mid-twentieth-century scholars, Thomas S. Kuhn and Leon Festinger, and two late nineteenth-century scholars, William James and Sigmund Freud, explains why.

Thomas S. Kuhn: Paradigms and Normal Science

In 1962 Thomas Kuhn argued in *The Structure of Scientific Revolutions* that scientists routinely limit their interest to natural phenomena that can be explained by extending or modifying the general theories that underlie the field of study with which the phenomena are associated.[109] Kuhn called these general theories "paradigms." Simultaneously restrictive and liberating, paradigms focus attention on problems that intelligent people can solve with the tools of their scientific specialty.

Kuhn compared scientific problems to crossword puzzles because the rules are clear and yet the solution requires patience and specialized knowledge. During periods of what Kuhn called "normal science," scientists apply existing general theories like Newtonian mechanics or Mendelian genetics to explain more and more of the phenomena of the natural world. But "scientific revolutions" in Kuhn's title shows his interest in the transition between normal science under the influence of one general theory and a competing later theory—for example, the transition from Newtonian mechanics to special relativity.

Kuhn wrote that normal science becomes less structured and less effective during scientific revolutions. An "essential tension" exists between the general theory and the phenomena that cannot be explained by that theory. As more phenomena are investigated, the old theory explains the new observations less well. Old observations that were discrepant with the theory but were ignored become more salient as they are repeated and verified by more researchers. When this happens, the original theory may have to be changed to accommodate the new observations, and it becomes a less consistent and less satisfying explanation of nature. Alternative theories are suggested, and if a new general theory (paradigm)

　　　　　　　　　　UFOs, ETs, and Alien Abductions

is proposed that explains both the old and the new observations, it will be accepted.[110]

Kuhn insists that ". . . there is no such thing as research in the absence of any paradigm. *To reject one paradigm without simultaneously substituting another is to reject science itself*" [my italics]. Kuhn even suggests that "some men have undoubtedly been driven to desert science because of their inability to tolerate crisis . . . that rejection of science in favor of another occupation is, I think, the only sort of paradigm rejection to which counter-instances by themselves can lead."[111]

If Kuhn is right, what does it mean for scientists' attitudes toward UFO phenomena? The answer is that, as David Jacobs noted in 1975, within "normal science," UFO reports have to be explained as phenomena from the fields of atmospheric physics, engineering, or psychology.[112] To use J. Allen Hynek's classification scheme (see pages 58–59), "nocturnal lights" must be misperceptions of stars or planets caused by a well-known visual phenomenon called autokinesis, in which stationary objects in a uniform field appear to move. A variety of nocturnal phenomena have been used to explain the appearance of UFOs over the years: Philip Klass said they were "ball lightning"; Donald Menzel, mirages; and psychologist Michael Persinger blamed "piezoelectric discharges." Menzel explained Hynek's "daylight discs" as optical phenomena (sun dogs). Radar-visual sightings were explained as temperature inversions and mirages. UFO close encounter reports by groups or individuals were the result of mutual suggestibility and sensation-seeking or psychopathology (hallucinations). Interest in UFOs was explained in the cultural context of myth and folklore, and the cultural explanation was the paradigm that included all of the motivations that led people to believe other people's stories about UFOs.

The conventional scientific attitude was summarized succinctly by Michael Shermer, founding publisher of *Skeptic* magazine and columnist for *Scientific American*:

> In all fields of science there is a residue of anomalies unexplained by the dominant theory. That does not mean the

prevailing theory is wrong or that alternative theories are right. It just means that more work needs to be done to bring those anomalies into the accepted paradigm. In the meantime, it is okay to live with the uncertainty that not everything has an explanation.[113]

The key to Shermer's thinking, and the key to all conventional scientific thinking, as Kuhn realized a half-century ago, is summarized in Shermer's phrase: "It just means that more work needs to be done to bring those anomalies into the accepted paradigm." The existing paradigm constrains normal science, regardless of the evidence!

UFO evidence cannot trigger a real paradigm shift, because *no physical theory published in the open literature explains how UFOs work.* In complete conformity with Kuhn's idea that "once it has achieved the status of paradigm, a scientific theory is declared invalid only if an alternate candidate is available to take its place," UFO phenomena will for the foreseeable future be seen by scientists as a puzzle to be explained by reference to atmospheric, meteorological, or psychological processes. Barring a dramatic, attention-riveting change in the UFO phenomenon, or an even more unlikely change in scientific attitudes, scientists will not agree that UFOs are real until there is an accepted theory about how to make a machine that will do what UFOs have repeatedly been seen to do. Until then, the scientific community will always say it is "premature" to so much as acknowledge the existence of facts that no theory can explain.[114]

• • •

Eighteenth- and nineteenth-century scientists spent much of their time making observations and collecting specimens that documented both the curiosities and the regularities of nature.[115] However, some twentieth-century philosophers of science have argued that collecting things or observing phenomena and then reasoning inductively from them is not really science.[116] Studying novel but unexplainable phenomena is certainly a professional blind alley

UFOs, ETs, and Alien Abductions

for any modern scientist whose livelihood depends on government research grants and scientific establishment support. Since no current scientific paradigm can explain the UFO evidence, no scientific funding agency will support UFO research—except as a study of psychological abnormality.

While our knowledge of nature is never complete, establishment scientists have faith that science advances by steps that are consistent with Kuhn's description of the progress of scientific revolutions. As paradigms grow stale and new ones develop, facts that fit neither the old paradigm nor the developing new one are not treated as scientific facts at all. Certainly the data that help shape a new paradigm will be fully weighed and considered, but, according to Kuhn, *there is no place in science for facts that can neither be explained under the old paradigm, nor that contribute to building a new paradigm.* Modern scientists are among those least likely to accept and accommodate facts that have no place in currently evolving theories of nature. In fact, they are trained to disregard anomalies like the evidence about UFOs and close encounters.

William James:
The Conservative Pleasure of Science

The nineteenth-century American psychologist William James also characterized scientific thinking as a process so conservative that it may lead to ignoring phenomena that just don't fit:

> The aim of "Science" is to attain conceptions so adequate and exact that we shall never need to change them. There is an everlasting struggle in every mind between the tendency to keep unchanged, and the tendency to renovate, its ideas. . . . Every new experience must be disposed of under some old head. The great point is to find the head which has to be least altered to take it in. Certain Polynesian natives, seeing horses for the first time, called them pigs, that being the nearest head. . . . Most of us grow more and more enslaved

to the stock conceptions with which we have once become familiar, and less and less capable of assimilating impressions in any but the old ways. . . . Objects which violate our established ideas of "apperception" are simply not taken account of at all; or, if on some occasion we are forced by dint of argument to admit of their existence, twenty-four hours later the admission is if as it were not, and every trace of inassimilable truth has vanished from our thought. Genius, in truth, means little more than the faculty of perceiving in an unhabitual way.

We feel neither curiosity nor wonder concerning things so far beyond us that we have no concepts to refer them to or standards by which to measure them. The Fuegians, in Darwin's voyage, wondered at the small boats but took the big ship as a "matter of course." Only what we partly know already inspires us with a desire to know more.[117]

This is Kuhn's twentieth-century argument expressed in nineteenth-century prose. Despite NASA engineer Paul Hill's ingenious speculations, modern science cannot explain how UFOs got here or how they maneuver once they are here. UFOs are not even partly understood, so they provide no scientific inspiration to learn more about them. The student of UFOs and close encounters gathers facts and systematizes them without the imprimatur of a scientific paradigm and, in fact, without any support from organized science.

Leon Festinger's Theory of Cognitive Dissonance

Twentieth-century American psychologist Leon Festinger developed a theory about thinking that was so simple your grandmother would have understood it.[118] (In the trade, we call this "grandmother psychology.") Festinger's theory of cognitive dissonance is based on the assumption that it is emotionally upsetting to hold simultaneous contradictory ideas. Festinger wondered what happens to those ideas as a result of the contradiction.

Suppose, for example, that Mary thinks Alice is her best friend. Then Mary hears from Sarah that Alice said mean things about her. That is contradictory, because best friends don't say mean things about each other. The heart of Festinger's theory is his insight into how people deal with the contradiction. If the contradiction is not central to your emotional life, it will not have much effect on your ideas or your behavior. But Alice is important to Mary. Her friendship matters, which means that Mary will have to change her mind about something concerning Alice. The first and most obvious thing to change is Mary's opinion that Alice is her friend. Saying mean things about a friend is a big negative; shouldn't that be enough to end Mary's friendship with Alice? Perhaps not. If there are a lot of plusses on the side of Mary staying friends with Alice, there are other things Mary can do to resolve the contradiction. One of them is to discount the truth of the observation. If Sarah is not as important to Mary as Alice, then Mary may decide that Sarah had a self-interested motive for telling Mary something about Alice that was untrue. Mary will change her opinion about Sarah and the evidence, and not about Alice, thus saving her friendship with Alice and denying the relevance of what she heard from Sarah. Another way of saving Mary's friendship with Alice is for Mary to trivialize what Sarah told her by reducing its apparent importance. She could tell herself, "Alice is always making jokes; I'm sure whatever she said was meant as a joke." These mental ploys succeed in saving Mary's friendship with Alice at the expense of Sarah's reputation and/or the validity or importance of what Mary heard from her. Festinger and his students studied the ways one could save a very important idea by changing less important ideas around it to reduce the dissonance between them.

Festinger's cognitive dissonance theory is central to understanding how the scientific community has responded to UFO and close encounter evidence. Imagine yourself a scientific professional, a close friend of "normal science." If I intrude on that friendship by presenting you with evidence related to your work that does not fit an established paradigm, I am compelling you to save your friendship with normal science by regarding my new evidence the same way Mary treated Sarah's story when it intruded on her friendship with Alice. One way to discredit my evidence and save your friendship with normal science would be to decide that I have ulterior motives or that I am unreliable, so in either case what I report does not have to be believed. If you can convince yourself that I am not really a scientist but instead a "wacko," a "contactee," or a "believer," my message becomes unreliable and my audience becomes contemptible. If you decide to make these mental adjustments instead of accepting the evidence, then your friendship with "normal science" remains intact. This cognitive dissonance response to UFO evidence was evident in the remarks made by Edward U. Condon, the director of the Air Force's Committee on Unidentified Flying Objects (see pages 46–47).

Sigmund Freud: Repression and Sublimation

Sigmund Freud thought that neuroses were caused by the mental effort required to repress emotionally unacceptable thoughts from one's consciousness.[119] Dissociative disorder is the modern name for the condition in which memory of traumatic events does not reach consciousness. Freud thought that repression had another effect: "sublimation."[120] Sublimation means turning the "psychic energy" generated by repressing thoughts into safer and less troublesome channels, and, as Freud put it "no small enhancement of mental capacity results from a predisposition which is dangerous as such."[121] While Freud believed repression and sublimation controlled dangerous hostility or sexual desires, psychologists now recognize that repression (or dissociation), and its result, sublimation, can result from a wider range of dangerous or upsetting ideas.

According to Freud, repressing a dangerous idea may lead to activity in a safer direction. What could a scientist with a repressed or dissociated awareness of UFO evidence do that would safely discharge the "psychic energy" generated by that hidden and forbidden knowledge, and, at the same time, create "no small enhancement in mental capacity"? The answer: carry out a search for extraterrestrial intelligence!

The search for extraterrestrial intelligence (SETI) is a scientific activity that uses radio telescopes to collect the multiple sources of radiation reaching the Earth from the rest of the universe.[122] SETI scientists then borrow spare cycles on networked computers to process those radiation inputs and filter out "intelligent signals from outer space."[123] SETI is respectable because it borrows the credibility of radio astronomy, whose intellectual bona fides are unimpeachable. I think many SETI researchers and supporters are motivated by their dissociated awareness that UFO evidence supports the extraterrestrial hypothesis, but as scientists without a supporting paradigm and as humans who, as Festinger theorized, work to avoid cognitive dissonance, the only thing they can do about that dissociated awareness is sublimate it by using the acceptable tools of their trade to support a harmless, respectable and marginally useful scientific activity.

The Escape to Popular Culture

Because the evidence that some UFOs are extraterrestrial vehicles is not part of an existing or emerging paradigm, because it is cognitively dissonant with normal science, because it has been either assimilated into the scientifically familiar or ignored completely, or because the evidence has been repressed and sublimated, the evidence that supports the existence of extraterrestrial travel has been written out of establishment science. The practicing mainstream scientist sees that UFO accounts are a part of popular culture and thinks that the correct pigeonhole for UFO and abduction accounts is not physical science, but folklore. Books, TV, and fictitious films based on UFO and alien themes are widespread in popular culture. The facts about UFOs and close encounters are found *only* in popular culture, because neither elite scientific culture (e.g. *Science, Nature*) nor elite general culture (e.g. *The New York Times*) provides a vehicle for UFO research and scholarship. Having been excluded from elite scientific and general culture, UFO and close encounter researchers and scholars must publish their findings where and when they can.[124]

Thomas E. Bullard pointed out that popular culture has been a repository for facts long before they are recognized by elite culture.[125] Bullard showed that UFO and close encounter facts are consistent across reports and form a coherent body of knowledge.[126] His conclusion deserves attention.

> UFOs qualify as folklore simply because they belong to unofficial culture, that body of beliefs held against and in spite of the denials of UFOs by government and scientific authorities. The observers, the experiments, maintain a stubborn opposition and even continue to see what should not exist to be seen, so they constitute a folk group and preserve their unofficial knowledge as the lore of the group. Contrary to a popular image, folklore is not necessarily false. The old weather sign of a ring around the moon as harbinger of rain has a perfectly good meteorological basis, and folklore recognized ball lightning long before science lent its stamp of approval. In principle, UFOs could be everything ufologists claim and still be folklore as well.[127]

The scientist who dismisses UFO evidence because it is "folklore" is putting facts into the wrong pigeonhole. J. Allen Hynek, who wrote the first systematic study of the UFO phenomenon in 1972, reminded us that today's scientific impossibility may be tomorrow's scientific commonplace:

> The frequently reported presence of "humanoids" capable of moving about in comfort in our highly restrictive terrestrial environment, and their association with "craft," exhibiting at times near-zero inertial mass yet able to leave physical traces of their presence is certainly a phenomenon beyond the pale of mid-twentieth–century physics. But there will surely be, we hope, a twenty-first century science and a thirtieth century science, and perhaps they will encompass the UFO phenomenon as twentieth century science has encompassed

the aurora borealis, a feat unimaginable to nineteenth century science, which likewise was incapable of explaining how the sun and stars shine.[128]

Establishment scientists do not have the resilience to acknowledge that some reliable instrumental records and human observations are caused by extraterrestrial vehicles and by extraterrestrials. When a UFO case attracts enough public attention, a scientific spokesman often advances a specious conventional explanation. If a specious conventional explanation cannot be advanced, some scientific person is likely to remark that we don't have enough information to explain the anomaly but if we did, the anomaly would disappear.

Anomalous instrumental records and human observations caused by extraterrestrial vehicles and extraterrestrials have not disappeared. During the half-century or more since government-supported science began to function less by observation and induction and more by the principles described by Kuhn, James, Festinger, and Freud, as outlined in this chapter, the scientific establishment has lost the ability to absorb, comprehend, and respond to anomalous data. This means that the recognition of, and response to, the presence of extraterrestrials will not be led by the government-supported scientific establishment. It will be led by people whose curiosity about the natural world has not been curtailed by the excessive conservatism of modern science.

10

Extraterrestrial Politics

The first nine chapters of this book reviewed what is known about UFOs and extraterrestrials and how governments, the scientific establishment, and the public have responded to that knowledge. An effective response to any change in our understanding about the world—whether it is the natural world (global warming) or the social world (the Arab spring) requires thought and discussion. Recognizing that extraterrestrials have been here dramatically changes what we know about both the natural world and the social world. This chapter reviews what has already happened in response to these changes and considers what more we—as citizens who are ultimately responsible for our government's policies—should insist be done about them.

Who Knows What?

There are private UFO investigation groups in forty-one countries, and there is often more than one group per country (the United States, for example, has more than fifty).[129] These groups collect information about UFO sightings or close encounters, investigate when time and resources permit, and catalog or report their work in a publication or on a website.

Public and private UFO research groups are active in Europe. The French government has a UFO research group within their space program (GEIPAN), and UFO documents are accessible on a public website. The Belgian government carried out a thorough investigation of low-level close encounters during 1989–1990 and published the results. The British Ministry of Defence recently uploaded its UFO-related documents to a public website.[130] The Russian government has unsystematically released UFO files from various government agencies, many dating from the Soviet era.[131] These governments, along with the governments of Brazil, Chile, Mexico, and Peru have said to the public, "Here's what we know. We don't know what to make of it."[132] They have shown us *some* of what they know, but we don't know whether they have shown us *everything*.

Government Secrets

The US Air Force website denies that UFOs are extraterrestrial, denies that they are technologically advanced, and denies that they are a threat to the security of the United States, and the Air Force has been saying that since 1970.[133] The Air Force states that it has not collected UFO data since Project Blue Book closed in 1970, but that is not true. There is a defense department form authorized under directive JANAP 146(B) for reporting anomalous aerial events to government military and security agencies.[134] This directive was first issued in 1949 and its later revisions are still in force.

Although the Air Force website says that "nothing has occurred that would support a resumption of UFO investigations by the Air Force," this does not mean that no UFO projects exist either within the Air Force or within other government agencies. It is easy to conceal government-sponsored research and development because there are many levels of security classification within the military-industrial complex. While I was a graduate student at Cornell University I worked summers and part-time for IBM's Federal Systems Division in Owego, New York, helping to develop radar navigation displays for the B-52 bomber. My security classification was Secret (between "Classified" and "Top Secret"). I had access to

UFOs, ETs, and Alien Abductions

Secret material, and I worked on projects whose details I was forbidden to divulge. In addition to the restriction based on security classification level, there is a general restriction based on the "need to know." You cannot read just any classified documents at your security level; you can only read documents containing information you "need to know" to work on your project.

That is not the whole secrecy story. Bernard Haisch, an astrophysicist who has edited a major astrophysical journal and participated in many US-funded satellite development programs, explained how the US government conceals research and development work from Congress and the public through Unacknowledged Special Access Programs (USAPs), or Black Projects.[135] For example, the government may begin to work with an aerospace contractor on a publicly acknowledged, innocuous-sounding research or development project; let's call it "upper atmosphere research devices." The contractor makes progress and meets a few preliminary milestones—enough to satisfy the government that the contractor is on the right track to develop a fast, high-altitude reconnaissance aircraft. The government then pays the remaining contract costs and terminates the contract only to revive it again, but this time as an Unacknowledged Special Access Program. Only four congressmen—the chairmen of the House and Senate Military Affairs and Appropriations Committees—even know the *names* of the black programs—and they are given no program details.

The Black Project does not publicly exist: the contractor and contractor employees are required to deny the existence of the program, and inquiries about "upper atmosphere research devices" are answered by pointing to the available contract documents which show that the contract has ended. Knowledge about the project is so restricted that even the heads of major military or intelligence departments may not know about it. According to Haisch, unacknowledged projects like this are "born secret" and cannot be disclosed even to the president. This high level of secrecy was established under laws dating from the early Cold War that were intended to protect atomic secrets.

This does not mean that the US government *is* involved in research or development concerning the UFO and close encounter phenomena. All it means is that *if* it is, the government doesn't have to tell you about it.

Roswell

The coffee cup that holds my pencils was bought by a traveling niece in a souvenir shop in Roswell, New Mexico.[136] A headline from the *Roswell Daily Record* of Tuesday, July 8, 1947, is printed on it: "RAAF [Roswell Army Air Force] Captures Flying Saucer on Ranch in Roswell Region." On June 24, 1947, Kenneth Arnold flew over the Cascade Mountains in Washington State, saw UFOs, and made "flying saucers" headline news. The Roswell "capture," two weeks later, is the index case for the US government's direct involvement with UFOs. Unlike the Kenneth Arnold sighting, the Roswell event is not a straightforward account of something seen by eyewitnesses and reported soon afterward. The crash narrative has been assembled from a tangle of information, disinformation, and speculation. It has taken a half-dozen investigators more than sixty years to find and collate the facts, and they still disagree about some of the details.

On Thursday July 3, 1947, W. W. "Mack" Brazel, foreman of the Foster Ranch near Corona, New Mexico, was riding over the ranch when he discovered an area about 200 to 300 feet wide and three-quarters of a mile long, oriented northwest to southeast, densely covered with irregular pieces of strange material. There was a shallow new gouge in the ground along the same axis about 500 feet long and ten feet wide, starting at the northwest corner of the debris field. The debris included very thin, parchment-like sheets that were so strong they could not be bent or cut. There was also foil-like material which, if crumpled, smoothed out again by itself. There were pieces of what appeared to be metal with some plastic properties. The metal was light, dull gray and non-reflective. It could not be cut or burned. Hammering did not deform it. There was also something that looked like nylon monofilament fishing line. There were small, flexible, and strong I-beams covered with symbols. The material was so thick on the ground that Brazel's sheep would not cross the littered area.

Brazel picked up some of the material and a few days later showed it to his nearest neighbors, who declined his offer to ride out and look at the rest of the debris. They suggested instead that he take some of it to the county seat at Roswell. Brazel had already driven into Corona and mentioned the debris to a brother-in-law, who told him about the "flying saucers." (Brazel had neither a phone nor a radio at his simply furnished ranch house; his wife and children lived in Tularosa, New Mexico, where the children went to school.) The brother-in-law also suggested that he take the material to Roswell.

On Sunday, July 6, when he had some free time, Brazel drove the seventy-five miles from the Foster Ranch to Roswell. He showed the material to Sheriff George A. Wilcox, who called the Roswell Army Air Force Base. Colonel William H. Blanchard, the base commander, Major Jesse Marcel, the intelligence officer of the 509th bomb group, and Captain Sheridan Cavitt, an officer from the Counter Intelligence Corps, showed up at the sheriff's office shortly afterward. Blanchard notified 8th Air Force Headquarters in Fort Worth, Texas about the find, and, acting on instructions from them, put some of the material in a bag and sent it by air to Fort Worth. Blanchard ordered Marcel and Cavitt to go back to the ranch with Brazel and inspect the debris field.

It was evening when they arrived at the ranch, so they slept overnight in an outbuilding and started their inspection the next day. They spent all day filling Marcel's Buick and Cavitt's jeep carryall with material, and then they drove back to the RAAF Base. Marcel went home at 2:00 in the morning and woke up his wife and eleven-year-old son to show them some of the material, which he spread out on the kitchen floor. His son, Dr. Jesse Marcel Jr., Army colonel, physician, and helicopter pilot, remembers the material well.

At 6:00 the next morning, Marcel and Cavitt went to Colonel Blanchard's house to show him what they had found. Blanchard realized, as did Major Marcel and the intelligence agent, that the debris was "not of this earth." He moved the daily staff meeting up to 7:30 a.m. instead of the usual 9:00 a.m. to deal with the situation and sent military police to the debris field to keep civilians away. He also organized a team of searchers to retrieve as much of the material as they could find, load it into trucks, and return it to the RAAF Base. At the same time, acting on the possibility that whatever accident had generated the debris field might also have led to a crash, he ordered an aerial search of the surrounding countryside.

Blanchard, solicitous of the good relationship between the people of Roswell and the RAAF Base and aware that Sheriff Wilcox and many others already knew about the strange material, had his public information officer draft a press release for local newspapers and radio stations which went from Roswell over the press wires to the world (and eventually to my coffee cup). It read in part:

> The many rumors regarding the flying discs became a reality yesterday when the intelligence office of the 509th Bomb Group of the Eighth Air Force, Roswell Army Air Field, was fortunate enough to gain possession of a disc through the cooperation of one of the local ranchers and the Sheriff's office of Chaves County.
>
> The flying object landed on a ranch near Roswell sometime last week. Not having phone facilities, the rancher stored the disc until such time as he was able to contact the sheriff's office, who in turn notified Major Jesse A. Marcel, of the 509th Bomb Group Intelligence Office.

An official "flying saucer" press release from the US Army Air Force, coming just two weeks after the Kenneth Arnold sighting, meant that the phones in Roswell newspaper and radio offices, Sheriff Wilcox's office, and the RAAF Base kept ringing for days.

Major Marcel was dispatched on a B-29 to Fort Worth with more of the material that had been brought back from the debris field. He was told to show it to Brigadier General Roger Ramey, Commander of the 8th Air Force, and then to fly it on to Wright-Patterson Field in Dayton, Ohio, where the Air Force's technical departments were located. Plans changed when Marcel arrived at Fort Worth. He took some of the material to General Ramey's office and spread it out on the floor. Ramey took him out of the office and into a nearby room where Marcel showed him the location of the debris field on a map. When Marcel and Ramey returned to the general's office, the debris was gone and the damaged remains of a weather balloon and its attached radar reflector had been substituted in its place. The General told Marcel "Don't say anything; I'll take care of this." A newspaper photographer was brought in, and General Ramey, his assistant, Colonel Thomas DuBose, Major Marcel, and Warrant Officer Irving Newton, who was a weather specialist, all posed with the balloon debris while Ramey told the photographer that they were looking at the weather balloon found at the Foster Ranch. Other newspaper and radio reporters were shown the balloon and told the same story.

Meanwhile, in Roswell, military personnel visited all of the media outlets that had received the "flying saucer" press release and demanded it back. They got them back. Mack Brazel had gone to the crash site with the recovery teams, but he returned to Roswell soon afterward and was interviewed by the owner and manager of a local radio station before the Air Force could intervene. The station owner was called from Washington, DC by both Nevada Senator Dennis Chavez and a Federal Communications Commission official and warned not to broadcast the interview. Brazel himself was held incommunicado in the RAAF Base "guest house" for six days, after which he left the base accompanied by Army personnel and visited the radio station that had interviewed him. He told them that his earlier story about the debris field was mistaken. He now said he had found a weather balloon and had brought the balloon to Sheriff Wilcox's office in Roswell. A news office in Albuquerque tried to send a teletype story based on the original press release, but the transmission was interrupted and a return transmission from the FBI warned them not to send the story.

The aerial search located a damaged UFO some distance southeast of the debris field.[137] Humanoid bodies were found in or near the wreckage. This area was cordoned off, and the UFO wreckage and the bodies were moved by truck to RAAF Base. Over the next few days at least nine flights containing wreckage and bodies left Roswell for Los Alamos via Kirtland Air Force Base in Albuquerque or for Wright-Patterson Field in Dayton.

Colonel Blanchard, the base commander, went on leave and was unavailable for further comment. Evening papers to the west of Roswell carried the original "flying saucer" press release, but the next morning the national and international press carried photographs of General Ramey, Major Marcel, and other officers with the weather balloon scraps along with the story that the "crashed disc" was simply a misidentified weather balloon with an aluminum-foil radar target attached. A typical news headline read: "General Ramey Empties Roswell Saucer."[138]

That was the immediate end of the Roswell story. There was no public interest in the story for the next thirty years. The right to deny information includes the freedom to confuse people about it; as Winston Churchill said, "In war-time, truth is so precious that she should always be attended by a bodyguard of lies." The US government, a Cold War antagonist, protected everything it knew about the Roswell crash behind barriers of secrecy and disinformation.

Investigating Roswell

Unverifiable rumors followed the crash at Roswell. The multiyear investigation that went beyond the rumors and traced witnesses, collated stories, and established the time line of the events that were described here began in 1977. Stanton Friedman, a nuclear physicist by training and a widely traveled UFO researcher and lecturer, was having coffee with the director of a Louisiana TV station in advance of an interview about an upcoming lecture. The director suggested that Friedman get in touch with a local ham radio buddy of his who had told the director that he had once handled material from a crashed flying saucer. The buddy was now-retired Jesse Marcel. Friedman phoned Marcel, who outlined his part of the story that was narrated here. But this was just one statement by one person, and Friedman had no reliable background information on Marcel.

Other pieces of the story of the crashed flying saucer in New Mexico began to accumulate from comments made to Friedman after his lectures. William L. Moore, an interested amateur, found original newspaper stories about the Roswell events in an archive at the University of Minnesota. They confirmed that Marcel was an Air Force veteran and that he was involved with the Roswell case. The newspaper leads, plus the accounts that Friedman had picked up during his lecture tours, were the nucleus of a long investigation during which many participants in the Roswell events were located and interviewed. *The Roswell Incident*, the first book published about the Roswell crash, was written by William Berlitz and William L. Moore with assistance from Stanton Friedman. It appeared in 1980. Later research filled in some gaps and corrected some inaccuracies in this first book.

The Center for UFO Studies sponsored and partially financed an investigation carried out by Donald Schmitt and Kevin Randle. Schmitt was then CUFOS's director of field investigations, and Randle is a retired Air Force intelligence officer. Schmitt and Randle reinterviewed as many of the people contacted by Moore and Friedman as they could find, and they carried their investigation to Albuquerque, Corona, and Roswell. They visited and flew over the crash site and visited the old Air Force base. They interviewed many new witnesses among the children and relatives of people who were at the scene in 1947. They used library resources and the Freedom of Information Act to obtain as many government documents related to activities at Roswell in 1947 as were publicly available. Many data sources that they expected would have been routinely available, like staff rosters for air base facilities and organizations, were unavailable. They interviewed 182 people who were willing to be named, and more who were not, in the course of completing *UFO Crash at Roswell*, which appeared in 1991. Friedman's own book, *Crash at Corona,* written with UFO investigator Don Berliner, appeared in 1992.

During the 1990s, CUFOS published articles about the crash evidence and the Air Force's after the fact explanations of the 1947 events. Air Force explanations included the supposed recovery of heretofore secret large balloon arrays and the recovery of high-altitude crash test dummies released during survivability studies. None of the Air Force explanations match the timelines and the facts narrated in the Roswell accounts.

Friedman, Randle, and Schmitt shared their research results, and the three of them agree about the story as I have narrated it. Friedman also summarized evidence suggesting that a second saucer crashed several hundred miles west of the Corona crash site at about the same time. Ambiguities about the reliability of witnesses to the second crash site make that event less certain than the well-established narrative of the one-disc crash near Corona.

In 2009, Thomas J. Carey and Donald Schmitt authored a follow-up to *UFO Crash at Roswell* called *Witness to Roswell.* They found more witnesses, interviewed them where possible, and where this was not possible they interviewed friends and relatives who had heard the stories.[139]

Behind the Scenes

Who was in charge at Roswell? Certainly not Base Commander William Blanchard. His "flying saucer" press release was withdrawn and General Ramey's weather balloon story was invented shortly after the debris reached Washington, DC. Although RAAF Base personnel cleaned up the debris field, they had limited access to the crash site, and officers from Washington were flown in to supervise the retrieval of the saucer and the bodies. The War Department (as it was at the time) either had a decision-making organization in place to deal with "flying saucers" on the basis of previous knowledge—perhaps starting with Kenneth Arnold's sighting two weeks earlier—or they reacted immediately and set one up to deal with the Roswell crash.

The War Department began by vacuuming up every crumb of information about the Roswell crash from the public media and by persuading Mack Brazel to retract what he had already said about the debris. Witnesses told Friedman, Randle, and Schmitt that they had been chased away from the debris field and the crash site by military guards and that they had been warned to say nothing about what they might have seen. The FBI got involved and shut down a teletype transmission based on the earlier "flying saucer" press release. The transshipment of material and bodies from Roswell to Los Alamos and Wright-Patterson Field in Dayton, Ohio was done secretly. Lapses occurred because civilians and military personnel on the scene were not as persuaded by intimidation as they should have been and some people with stories to tell had never been reached by the military. Information leakage was diffuse and slow until 1977, when Jesse Marcel, who had retired from the Air Force with the rank of lieutenant colonel, was reached by Stanton Friedman.

Thomas DuBose and Arthur Exon, both retired Air Force brigadier generals, spoke to Randle and Schmitt about the Roswell events of 1947. DuBose, at that time a colonel and General Ramey's assistant, was one of the officers who posed with the weather balloon debris. He confirmed that General Ramey had received orders from Washington to provide a cover story. General Exon, a lieutenant colonel in 1947, was at Wright Field in Dayton when the material from Roswell began to arrive. He described test results at Wright Field that confirmed the general description given earlier: strong, light material, much of which could not be bent or broken. While at Wright Field Exon heard about a UFO oversight committee that was headed by the president. Its other twelve members were the military department cabinet members, the CIA director, and senior technical experts like the chief of the Air Material Command and the director of Air Intelligence. Exon thought the committee was assisted by a secretariat and its secret technical work was done by scientific and technical employees in various government departments. Exon was later assigned to the Pentagon, and eventually, as base commander, back to Wright-Patterson Air Force Base. Both in Washington and while in command back at Wright-Patterson, he dealt indirectly with activities he thought were organized and directed by the oversight committee.

A civilian group called the Joint Research and Development Board might have helped to organize the UFO oversight committee. It was organized under President Harry S. Truman to advise the executive branch about the conduct of military research. From 1946 to 1952 the board continued the tradition of civilian cooperation with the military's war effort that was so successful during World War II. Its executive secretary was Lloyd Berkner, a member of the 1952 CIA-organized Robertson Panel that recommended a government UFO debunking policy. The CIA panel chairman, Howard P. Robertson, was the director of the Defense Department's Weapons System Evaluation Group, which had been established by the Research and Development Board. The small group of senior scientists who helped the government in the immediate post-war period were the people most likely to be asked for advice about the security threat posed by technologically superior UFOs. But who the UFO overseers were then, and who they are now, is not known. It is one of the better-kept secrets of the US government.

It was many years after the event that researchers Friedman, Randle, and Schmitt found people who were willing to talk about the UFO crash and recovery at Roswell. Since then the British, Belgian, and French governments have made UFO information public. Perhaps because other governments have released UFO information, US government ex-employees and retired military officers are now more willing to talk about the UFOs they dealt with on their watch.[140]

Alaska UFO Sighting: 1986

In 1986 a Japan Air Lines Boeing 747 cargo jet was flying between Paris and Tokyo with a scheduled refueling stop in Anchorage,

Alaska. As it approached Anchorage the three-man crew saw an immense UFO, "as big as an aircraft carrier," rendezvous with and pace their aircraft for about a half hour. It flew, as UFOs always do, in ways that no terrestrial craft can fly. The UFO was tracked by FAA air traffic control radar as well as military radar. The sighting was discussed on the radio between the aircraft crew and the air traffic controllers.

When the story leaked out a few months later, the Anchorage FAA office called John J. Callahan, then chief of the FAA's Office of Accident Investigation and Prevention in Washington, to ask him how they should deal with the phone calls and media requests. This was the first Callahan had heard about the sighting. He told them to send him all of the radar and voice tapes from the event. He replayed the radar tapes along with the voice tapes in a radar simulator so he could see what the FAA traffic controllers had seen on radar while he listened to their conversation with the Japan Air Lines crew.

After briefing his FAA boss, Callahan was told to set up another briefing for the White House. He met with White House science advisers, CIA officials, FAA technicians, and military officers. When the briefing was over, the CIA took the tapes and told Callahan and the others that "this event never happened, we were never here. We're confiscating all this data, and you are all sworn to secrecy."[141] A government employee cannot casually demand secrecy from anyone on his own authority, and Callahan didn't take the CIA secrecy threat seriously: as soon as he retired he wrote about what had happened. Fewer people now feel constrained by government warnings about secrecy and fewer are worried by threats, because the facts about UFOs are so common that to demand secrecy will produce a "you must be kidding" reaction from the ever-increasing number of people in and out of government who know what they're looking at when they see a UFO.

Disinformation

UFOs and close encounters still attract contactees and "believers" so lacking in credentials or common sense that their very existence protects the phenomenon from serious study by the many people who trust their own common sense, value their own credentials, and distrust the crowd. It takes almost no effort to keep that fringe big enough and active enough to marginalize serious interest. But every now and then, the government steps in to make sure that the facts about UFOs and abductions remain tainted by overenthusiasm and credulity.

Paul Bennewitz

Paul Bennewitz was a scientifically trained businessman whose company supplied test equipment to Kirtland Air Force Base in Albuquerque, New Mexico. In the late 1970s he believed that he had detected electromagnetic radiations from UFOs and that he had seen and filmed UFOs flying near Kirtland. He brought this to the attention of the Air Force, which ignored him. He brought it to the attention of the Aerial Phenomenon Research Organization, which also ignored him, having decided that Bennewitz was mentally unstable. But in 1980 an Air Force agent, using William L. Moore, coauthor of *The Roswell Incident,* as a go-between, contacted Bennewitz and started to feed him a heavy diet of disinformation.

The agent claimed to represent a group of disaffected Air Force insiders who wanted to publicize the truth about UFOs, and through Moore he fed Bennewitz a paranoid nightmare of Alien–US government contact involving a hidden underground UFO base, exchanges with aliens on other planets (as, for example, in the Steven Spielberg movie *Close Encounters of the Third Kind*), and aliens being given permission to perform cattle mutilations, a phenomenon sometimes associated with UFOs, and to carry out other intrusive activities in exchange for advanced technical information. Bennewitz swallowed this information and it eventually swallowed him, sending him to the insane asylum before he died in 2005.

Linda Moulton Howe

The disinformation campaign then switched from Bennewitz to documentary filmmaker and UFO researcher Linda Moulton Howe, who, unlike amateur investigator William L. Moore, was a victim and not an accomplice. She had already investigated cattle mutilations and had begun to plan a documentary on UFOs for HBO. The same Air Force investigator who contacted Bennewitz contacted her and invited her to Kirtland Air Force Base, where she was shown, but not allowed to keep, a document purporting to be a presidential briefing paper. It outlined a number of UFO crashes including the Roswell crash, described the usual type of humanoid, and discussed other UFO-related research projects and alien contacts both current and historical. She contacted HBO, but HBO was suspicious and wanted some kind of agreement in writing from the allegedly disaffected government agents. Delay followed delay; HBO got cold feet, the documentary was canceled, and Howe got nothing after having been tantalized with the promise of more. She realized that she was being sold a bill of goods and dropped the contact. She kept her sanity, but a potentially interesting documentary was scuppered by the disinformation-and-delay campaign to which she was subjected.

Another piece of disinformation turned up as a roll of exposed 35 mm film in a documentary film producer's mailbox. The producer was working on a movie with the same William L. Moore who fed disinformation to Paul Bennewitz. The exposed film showed an eight-page document about the government oversight committee that retired Brigadier General Arthur Exon had also heard of. There was a briefing memo for President Dwight D. Eisenhower when he took office in 1952, another memo from President Truman establishing the UFO oversight committee in 1947, a roster of members' names, and details about the Roswell crash and other UFO-related events. What makes the document a disinformation tool is that the details are plausible but the document is stylistically discrepant from the government bureaucratese of the day, and the Truman note has a signature that might have been copied from another letter.

As intended, the documents set off an uproar among the researchers and scholars who pay attention to UFOs, and it poisoned all of the information it contained for anyone with legitimate credentials who was watching the confusion from outside. When you mix tainted information with facts, the facts become tainted as well, which is the goal of successful disinformation. Disinformation was used twice in the 1980s by the same Air Force agent, and twice by a former UFO researcher whose role as a conduit for disinformation may have helped to push one of his victims into insanity.[142]

The weak point of disinformation is that once you identify it as such, it tells you that something important is being hidden. In the case of Bennewitz, it suggests that the Air Force was disinforming him about technological developments related to UFOs (perhaps reverse engineering based on the Roswell recovery, many years before) and possibly disinforming him about recent close encounters near military facilities in the southwest. In the case of Linda Moulton Howe, it suggests disinformation about cattle mutilations (a subject not considered in this book, but possibly UFO-related and interesting in its own right) and government oversight of the UFO phenomenon. And with respect to the briefing documents and roster for a UFO oversight organization, it suggests that such an organization exists and that its structure and purpose bear some relationship to what was described in the disinformation documents, whose purpose was to poison public opinion against the very idea that such an organization exists.

UFOs and Government

One role of government is to protect us from each other, which is why we have police, laws, and courts and why governments sign treaties to regulate citizens' behavior across national borders. Viola-

UFOs, ETs, and Alien Abductions

tions of citizens' rights within the nation are settled by law; across national borders, they are settled by treaty, diplomacy, or war. Force is the ultimate arbiter of domestic disagreements between citizens (through the actions of the police and the courts), and it is the ultimate arbiter of disagreements between nations.

Kidnapping is a crime, and abduction by extraterrestrials is kidnapping. Alien abductions erode the personal protection that Americans expect from their government. International treaties regulate commercial aviation, and this authority is undercut when large, low-flying objects hover over countryside, roads, towns, and cities and come and go at will across national boundaries without filing flight plans, communicating with air traffic controllers, operating in established airways, respecting operational ceilings, or displaying correct running lights. UFOs do not respect domestic law or international treaties, and governments have every reason to prevent low-altitude surveillance and unauthorized, uncontrolled, and potentially dangerous airspace intrusion.

The response of all terrestrial governments to unauthorized UFO surveillance should be to develop deterrents that can control UFOs in national airspace in order to maintain protection against domestic trespassing by extraterrestrials and to maintain aviation safety. Deterrence does not mean shooting down UFOs with bullets or missiles; that has been tried and it does not work. It means developing weapons that *could* damage or destroy UFOs and then demonstrating that the weapons are ready for use. If we cannot duplicate UFO aerospace technology, then we should at least learn to defend against it. Terrestrial governments will then be able to negotiate on more equal footing with extraterrestrials whose technology is better than ours.

If effective deterrence is still a distant goal, then a response that was followed openly by the Belgian government in 1989–1990 and is now followed surreptitiously by the US Air Force is the right policy: scramble fighter jets and chase UFOs away from population centers and military installations. Apparently, UFO pilots aren't looking for a confrontation, and they usually leave when chased. This approach is not so much aggressive as it is admonitory. It is more or less like a small dog barking loudly when the postman rings the doorbell. Both the dog and the postman know that there is bluffing involved in the confrontation, but the postman also knows that he has been put on notice—and one day, if he makes a false move, the dog might just try to take a piece out of his ankle.

Developing an effective defense may give us a chance to discover, as equals, what we can do for the extraterrestrials and what they can do for us. But with or without that defense we should make the extraterrestrials aware that although our intentions are not hostile, they are trespassing on our posted property without a permit. We should remind them of that whenever and wherever we can. If the trespassers turn out to be guests whom we are happy to welcome, so much the better. But if it turns out that they are unwelcome intruders, we should be prepared to deal with them as effectively as our technology permits, and we should encourage our scientists and engineers to get on with it.

Fear of Extraterrestrials

Two political scientists suggest that an unorganized conspiracy of like-minded people has banished the UFO phenomenon to the fringes of popular culture so that it does not disturb the authority of cultural elites.[143] Alexander Wendt and Raymond Duvall postulate that we stopped worshiping the natural forces that were once thought to control human destiny long ago. Instead, we transferred responsibility for our destiny to the institutions of government and civil society. Those institutions are administered by a meritocracy of capable people: the cultural elites.

Wendt and Duvall think that members of the cultural elite (and, I suppose, anyone else who thinks the same way) fear losing their control back to the "gods"—no longer the gods of hurricanes, earthquakes, and volcanoes, but to extraterrestrials, whose technology we can neither surpass nor control. Cultural leaders resist admitting the existence of extraterrestrials and extraterrestrial technology because

UFOs, ETs, and Alien Abductions

the admission would weaken the authority of human elites and the governments and institutions that they administer. That is why elite institutions actively marginalize UFO interest and why elite leaders object when someone tries to bring the UFO phenomenon back into mainstream culture.

The Wendt and Duvall theory is a perspicacious adaptation of Leon Festinger's cognitive dissonance theory introduced in chapter 9. Wendt and Duvall think elite culture is experiencing a kind of collective cognitive dissonance which is reduced by relegating the frightening idea of superior extraterrestrial technology to the fringe of cultural awareness. So long as UFOs and extraterrestrials are classified as figments of the popular imagination, the elites don't have to worry about them. This soothing oblivion is aided and abetted, Wendt and Duvall think, by the secrecy and disinformation practiced by people in positions of authority who know the facts but won't reveal them—and I agree with them.

The Spaniards and the Aztecs

Being visited by strangers with superior technology happened many times over on this planet during the European ages of exploration. Bearded Europeans with pale skin and light hair sailed their huge ships and carried their terrible weapons to lands whose people had never seen Europeans or their technology. With few exceptions, the Europeans did not treat their hosts well. The histories of Africa, Asia, and the Americas testify to the disruptive effect of those intrusions on local societies. A notable example is the fall of the Aztec empire in Mexico in 1521.

The Aztecs believed that the gods of the local cities they conquered had fled Mexico but would someday return. When the Aztec emperor Montezuma was told in 1519 that Hernán Cortés and his army of 600 Spanish soldiers had arrived on the coast of Mexico, Montezuma and his court thought that the Spaniards might be those gods. Spanish horses were like mythical beasts, Spanish armor was proof against Aztec arrows, and Spanish cannons were terrifyingly destructive. Montezuma was torn between hospitality and resistance, and his morale and that of his court was weakened by the mental conflict. The Spaniards were able to enlist local allies against the feared Aztecs, and after a long and fierce struggle, Cortés, his weapons, his soldiers, and his allies were able to destroy the Aztec empire based on the island city of Tenochtitlan (in the center of modern-day Mexico City).[144]

Superior technology alone did not bring down the Aztec empire. Demoralization and internal dissent combined to undermine resistance, while committed allies, a united population, and a strong government might have kept the Spaniards at bay.

Extraterrestrials and Public Policy

After the Second World War began in Europe, but well before the Japanese attacked Pearl Harbor and the Axis powers declared war against America, the Roosevelt administration started to rearm the United States, ship weapons and munitions to Great Britain, and use the US Navy to protect the convoys carrying those supplies across the Atlantic. There was a strong isolationist sentiment in the United States against any involvement in European affairs, and the Roosevelt administration's controversial policies were debated in newspaper editorials, on the radio, in public meetings, and in the US Congress. The public and legislative debates ended with Congress passing an increased defense budget and the Selective Service Act, which established a peacetime military draft, and the Lend-Lease Act, which provided aid on credit to Great Britain and other Allies.

Every aspect of American foreign policy in the years leading up to World War II was controversial and publicly debated—how could it be otherwise, in a country where the legislature and the executive are accountable to the people? But the details of American military preparation—what kinds of ships, planes, and tanks to build and what new weapons to develop—were not discussed or debated publicly because they were within the competence of the executive branch's War Department and Navy Department and revealing the details would have aided potential enemies.

Our planet has attracted the unanticipated and uninvited but well-documented attention of extraterrestrials. Some European and South American governments have made their UFO evidence available, while private organizations have provided much more. The US Air Force still denies that there is any evidence, but that is untrue.[145] The American government's attitude toward UFO evidence was set when UFOs started to arrive in large numbers at the beginning of the Cold War. UFO information was treated as a military secret, and, as explained in chapter 1, UFO observations were publicly dismissed because they interfered with the observer-based air defense system of the time.

Although the Cold War is over, not even the president has access to some national security information under the extremely restrictive atomic energy control legislation passed after World War II. The same laws prevent the release of UFO information. In 1997 the late American senators Daniel Patrick Moynihan and Jesse Helms tried to introduce a less restrictive secrecy bill. Moynihan cited the social scientist Max Weber, a student of the bureaucratic state, who wrote, "Bureaucratic administration always tends to be an administration of 'secret sessions'; insofar as it can, it hides its knowledge and action from criticism."[146] Moynihan and Helms got nowhere. It seems that, as Weber predicted, the people who can legally keep UFO secrets don't trust the rest of us. Astrophysicist Bernard Haisch quotes a US government intelligence official whose work involved the analysis of UFO-related technology:

The elite involved in the black programs are among the smartest people on the planet, but even so remain deeply puzzled by much of what they've learned. They tend to regard the public with disdain, like undisciplined and unruly children incapable of handling information of extraordinary complexity. While officially supporting democracy, the black program elite in reality espouse a kind of benevolent dictatorship or enlightened oligarchy by those, such as themselves, who have earned the right to know and to make decisions in the best interest of civilization, to which the ordinary person, being lazy and easily distracted, is not motivated or qualified to contribute anyway. The average American cares more about the Super Bowl than about life elsewhere in the Universe. The intellectual mentors of those with clout and power are Plato and Machiavelli, not Aristotle and Jefferson. Over the past 50 years, the highest courts have accepted and upheld the precedence of national security over the First and Fourth Amendments. So even if the public wanted to know, that would not constitute a legal need or right to know. The elite are doing their patriotic duty by trying to control the situation within the established rules of national security.[147]

No sane person wants or expects the executive branch to explain how to reverse engineer a UFO or build the weapons needed to regain control of our airspace. But applying military security standards to information that would enable the public to think clearly about extraterrestrials is a mistake. No one who respects our system of representative government can justify withholding from Congress and the public the knowledge that, as the Apollo 13 astronauts said when they contacted Houston, "we have a problem."[148] Like the debate about America's preparation for World War II, public policy about extraterrestrials should be discussed and decided on the basis of the facts. Private organizations know and have reported some of the facts. If private organizations with limited budgets and no access to high-tech surveillance equipment have uncovered some of the facts about UFOs, then the US government, with its extensive aerospace tracking and surveillance capability, must know a lot more. The executive branch persistently and ludicrously denies that there are any facts at all. The result is that neither Congress nor the people know whether they have enough information to begin considering the problem.

UFOs, ETs, and Alien Abductions

Congress should reopen the public debate about UFOs and extraterrestrials. America has the largest defense budget and the most powerful armed force on the planet. Smaller allies as well as the larger powers that have a distant but mutually respectful relationship with the United States will have little choice but to follow the lead of Congress in dealing with UFOs. Before it can act, Congress will have to repeal parts of the Atomic Energy Act of 1946 and its successor, the Atomic Energy Acts of 1954 and 1964, because those are the laws that authorize the Atomic Energy Commission to withhold information from anyone the Commission decides does not have a "need to know." When Congress finally gains access to and then disseminates the United States' nontechnical information about UFOs and close encounters, then we can have an informed debate about extraterrestrial surveillance. The goal should be to figure out how to maximize the benefit and minimize the disruption of this unsolicited interest in us and our planet.

What Happens Next?

UFOs might go away and not come back—at least not until many years have passed and the preoccupation with UFOs and ETs that began in the mid-twentieth century has faded. We do not understand or control the extraterrestrial agenda. If they go away, this book and its predecessors become anachronisms. The extraterrestrial hypothesis is so fraught with intellectual upheaval and potential danger that if reports of UFO sightings, close encounters, and abductions drop to and remain at zero then there will be a huge sigh of relief throughout the scientific and political world and the whole topic will be buried in oblivion.

It is hard to know what will happen next. H. A. L. Fisher, an English historian, wrote this in the introduction to *A History of Europe*, published in 1935:

Men wiser and more learned than I have discerned in history a plot, a rhythm, a predetermined pattern. . . . I can see only one emergency following upon another as wave follows upon wave, only one great fact with respect to which, since it is unique, there can be no generalizations, only one safe rule for the historian: that he should recognize in the development of human destinies the play of the contingent and the unforeseen. This is not a doctrine of cynicism or despair. The fact of progress is written plain and large on the page of history; but progress is not a law of nature. The ground gained by one generation may be lost by the next. The thoughts of men may flow into the channels which lead to disaster and barbarism.[149]

Nothing that has happened since he wrote those words contradicts his recognition of the uncertainty and unpredictability of human destiny.

A Final Word

Over the past half-century we have had intermittent contact with extraterrestrial civilization. We do not know the motives and cannot predict the future behavior of the extraterrestrials who observe us and who occasionally catch and release some of us to satisfy their curiosity about the predominant species on this planet. Whether they will continue to interact with us it is impossible to say; whether they will play a significant role in our future it is equally impossible to say.

There are psychological barriers to recognizing the straightforward facts about the extraterrestrial origin of UFOs and the direct involvement of extraterrestrials in human life, but the evidence is clear and people are beginning to understand it. This is largely due to the work of UFO researchers but it has been helped by the creativity of Hollywood. We imagine extraterrestrials as a part of the real world through our exposure to the fictional worlds of *Close Encounters of the Third Kind*, *District 9*, *E.T. the Extra-Terrestrial*, *Independence Day*, *Men in Black*, *Taken*, and *The X-Files*.

UFO researchers, who deal with facts, have a duty to guide the transition from the UFOs and ETs of Hollywood's imagination to the UFOs and ETs of reality. If big, low-flying UFOs do not force the issue by cruising slowly over large cities in daylight; if less spectacular reports of smaller daytime UFOs and nighttime close encounters continue as before, then UFO researchers must continue to give the public accurate information about the extraterrestrials who are watching us and occasionally interacting with us.

Political decisions in a free society command respect and generate action when they are informed by public discussion leading to a common understanding and a common vision. The goal of this book has been to present facts about UFOs and extraterrestrials that might lead to a common understanding and vision about the problems and opportunities that are imposed on us by the reality of extraterrestrial contact. My motivation is explained by an Old Testament proverb that is as true today as it was when it was recorded centuries ago: *Where there is no vision, the people perish.*

Acknowledgments

This book is based on the work and vision of many people, including Thomas E. Bullard, John Carpenter, Jerome Clark, George Eberhart, Stanton Friedman, David Gotlib, James Harder, Jan Harzan, Richard Haines, Bernard Haisch, Wido Hoville, David Jacobs, Leslie Kean, Bruce Maccabee, Kathleen Marden, Mark Rodeghier, Michael Swords, Ron Westrum, and Robert Wood.

I enjoyed debates with collegial skeptics Susan Clancy, Richard McNally, Leonard Newman, and Roger Pitman. I acknowledge with appreciation and respect the contributions of writers and researchers who I knew but are now gone: Stuart Appelle, C. D. B. Bryan, Budd Hopkins, J. Allen Hynek, and John Mack. I thank the directors and investigators of the UFO groups that keep us informed: MUFON, CUFOS, FUFOR, and IF. I also thank colleagues in UFO-Québec with whom I worked from 1968 through 1980.

I thank Ingrid Birker of the McGill University Faculty of Science for inviting me to give four lectures on UFOs and Abductions in January and February of 2010, and I thank Raj Ram for encouraging those lectures. The lectures were the starting point for this book.

I was able to follow the UFO story from 1947 to the present through Jerome Clark's *UFO Encyclopedia* and David Jacobs' *The UFO Controversy in America.* Jacobs edited *UFOs and Abductions: Challenging the Borders of Knowledge,* which contains historical chapters by many authors, all of whom are acknowledged above. James R. Lewis's *UFOs and Popular Culture* was useful, as was Leslie Kean's *UFOs: Generals, Pilots, and Government Officials Go On the Record.* Ray Fowler, Philip Imbrogno, Martin Jasek, Kevin D. Randle, Donald

R. Schmitt, John F. Schuessler, and Walter Webb wrote monographs on specific cases that were essential reading.

I thank Tim Deveaux, Dimitris Hatzopoulos, and Richard Klagsbrun for suggesting books I didn't know I needed until I read them.

I acknowledge the friendship and support of the late Budd Hopkins, and of Leslie Kean, for their interest in and advice about this book. I thank Stanton Friedman and Kathleen Marden for suggestions about the text, and Martin O'Malley and Carrie Bell for advice about titles and publicity. Douglas and Verna Donderi as well as David Jacobs, and Greg Brandenburgh and Susie Pitzen, editors with Hampton Roads Publishing, made valuable suggestions that improved the manuscript.

Above all I thank Verna, Andrea, and Douglas, whose love, common sense, and critical thinking kept me down to earth while exploring the extraterrestrial world. They make everything I do worthwhile.

Notes

1   J. Allen Hynek, Philip J. Imbrogno, and Bob Pratt, *Night Siege: The Hudson Valley UFO Sightings* (St. Paul, MN: Llewellyn, 1998).

2   Tracy Kidder, "Facts and the Nonfiction Writer," *The Writer* 107, no. 2 (1994), 14–17.

3   W. Hoville and D. C. Donderi, "RR2 au lac baskatong," UFO-Québec Informations, Recherches, 16, quatrième trimester (1978), 8–11.

4   See also Budd Hopkins, *Art, Life, and UFOs: A Memoir* (San Antonio, TX: Anomalist, 2009).

5   D. C. Donderi, "A Multidimensional Scaling Program for Distinctiveness and Similarity Based on Stimulus Classification and Information Measurement," *Behavior Research Methods, Instruments and Computers,* 29(4), (1997), 549–555.

6   Stuart Appelle, Don Donderi, J. Bellissimo, and Budd Hopkins, "Common Symbols Are Remembered by People Self-Reporting Alien Abductions" (San Francisco, CA: Association for Psychological Science, 2009). (poster)

7   *en.wikipedia.org/wiki/Index_case*

8   J. Clark, "Arnold Sighting," *The UFO Encyclopedia: The Phenomenon from the Beginning,* 2nd edition, vol. I: A–K, (1998), 139–143.

9   J. E. McDonald, "Science in Default: Twenty-Two Years of Inadequate UFO Investigations," in *UFOs: A Scientific Debate,* eds. Carl Sagan, and T. Page (New York: Barnes & Noble, 1972).

10   Edward J. Ruppelt, *The Report on Unidentified Flying Objects,* (New York: Ace Books, 1956).

11   *www.af.mil/information/factsheets/factsheet.asp?id=188*

12   Jerome Clark, "The Extraterrestrial Hypothesis in the Early UFO Age," in *UFOs and Abductions: Challenging the Borders of Knowledge,* ed. D. M. Jacobs (Lawrence, KS: University Press of Kansas, 2000), 122–140.

13   This history is outlined in Ruppelt's *The Report on Unidentified Flying Objects.*

14   Jerome Clark, *The UFO Encyclopedia,* vol. II (Detroit, MI: Omnigraphics, 1998), 243–254.

15   *The Complete Writings of Thucydides: The Peloponnesian War* (New York: Modern Library, 1934), 14.

16   Ruppelt, *The Report on Unidentified Flying Objects*, 186.

17   Ibid., 163.

18   The complete text of the Robertson Panel Report was found in the Air Technical Intelligence Center archives by Dr. James D. Macdonald, a scientific supporter of the extraterrestrial hypothesis (ETH).

19   Ruppelt, *The Report on Unidentified Flying Objects,* 186.

20   Clark, *The UFO Encyclopedia,* vol. II, 583–584.

21   Richard H. Hall, *The UFO Evidence* (Washington, DC: National Investigations Committee on Aerial Phenomena, 1964).

22   L. Davidson, *Flying Saucers: An Analysis of the Air Force Project Blue Book Special Report No. 14,* 3rd edition (Ramsey, NJ: Ramsey-Wallace Corp, 1966).

23   J. Allen Hynek, "Talk to the Hypervelocity Impact Conference Banquet, Elgin Air Force Base, April 27, 1960," National Archives Record NARA-PBB87-415, 1960.
      www.bluebookarchive.org/page.aspx?PageCode=NARA-PBB87-415

24   Don Berliner, Marie Galbraith, and Antonio Huneeus, *Unidentified Flying Objects Briefing Document: The Best Available Evidence* (UFO Research Coalition, 1995), 57.

25   Ibid., 59.

26   Jacobs, *The UFO Controversy in America,* 191.

27   It was the "saucer wave" of 1965, continuing into 1966, with these well-publicized sightings, that persuaded me to study both UFOs and the perceptual and motivational aspects of UFO reports.

28   Popular skepticism was reflected in lyrics to the Creedence Clearwater Revival song "It Came Out of the Sky".

29   David R. Saunders, and R. Roger Harkins, *UFOs? Yes!: Where the Condon Committee Went Wrong* (Toronto, Ontario: New American Library, 1968), Appendix A: 242–244.

30   David R. Saunders, and R. Roger Harkins, *UFOs? Yes!: Where the Condon Committee Went Wrong* (Toronto, Ontario: New American Library, 1968).
      Jerome Clark, "University of Colorado UFO Project," in *The*

UFO Encyclopedia, vol. II, (Detroit, MI: Omnigraphics, 1998), 946–959.

Jacobs, *The UFO Controversy in America.*

Michael D. Swords, "The University of Colorado UFO Project: The 'Scientific Study of UFOs.'" *Journal of UFO Studies,* New Series, 6, (1995/1996), 149–184.

31   E. U. Condon, *Scientific Study of Unidentified Flying Objects.* (New York: Bantam Books, 1969), 1–6.

32   *en.wikipedia.org/wiki/Project_Blue_Book*

33   *en.wikipedia.org/wiki/Occam's_razor*

34   R. V. Jones, *Most Secret War* (London: Hamish Hamilton, 1978), 564.

35   J. Allen Hynek, "UFOs Merit Serious Study," *Science,* 154, 3747 (1966), 329.

36   In fact, one secretary of the Air Force did see a UFO. So did President Jimmy Carter when he was Governor of Georgia. But both reports were of daylight disks, middling in strangeness. And since only one person, however reputable, described each sighting, the reports only count as middling in probability.

37   William Markowitz, "The Physics and Metaphysics of Unidentified Flying Objects," *Science,* 157, 3794 (1967), 1274–1279.

38   Donald I. Warren, "Status Inconsistency Theory and Flying Saucer Sightings," *Science,* 170, 3958 (1970), 599–603.

39   Ionized (electrically charged) gas glows as the excited electrons in the gas release light energy while relapsing to a less energetic state. This sometimes happens around power lines in humid or dusty weather, on ships' masts during misty or stormy weather ("Saint Elmo's fire"), or very occasionally even rolling down fireplace flues into living rooms during a thunderstorm.

40   A University of Chicago classmate (1952–1957).

41   Carl Sagan, *Broca's Brain: Reflections on the Romance of Science* (New York: Random House, 1974), 55.

42   Budd Hopkins, "Carl Sagan and Me," *International UFO Reporter,* 22 (2), (1997), 12.

43   Hynek, Imbrogno, and Pratt, *Night Siege,* 20–22.

44   Major General Wilfried De Brouwer, (Ret)., "The UAP Wave Over Belgium," in *UFOs: Generals, Pilots, and Government Officials Go On the Record,* Leslie Kean (New York: Harmony Books, 2010), 24–40.

45   Martin Jasek, MSc., PE, *Giant UFO in the Yukon Territory.* UFOBC Special Report No. 1 (Delta, British Columbia, Canada, 2000).

46   Glen Schulze and Robert Powell, "Stephenville Lights: A Comprehensive Radar and Witness Report Study Regarding the Events of January 8, 2008" (Fort Collins, CO: Mutual UFO Network, 2008), 47.

47   See, for example, Arthur M. Arkin, John S. Antrobus, and Steven J. Ellman's *The Mind in Sleep: Psychology and Psychophysiology,* 1st ed. (Hillsdale, NJ: Erlbaum, 1978), and J. Allan Hobson's *The Dreaming Brain* (New York: Basic Books, 1988).

48   Richard H. Hall, *The UFO Evidence, Volume II: A Thirty-Year Report* (Lanham, MD: Scarecrow Press, 2000).

49   Letter and report to NICAP, Washington, DC from C. R. Ricks, Idaho Falls, Idaho.

50   Yves Sillard, "Groupe d'Étude des Phénomènes Aérospatiaux Non-identifiés: Un Defi a la Science" (Paris: Le cherche-midi, 2007), 10.

51 See for example Hall, *The UFO Evidence, Volume II,* 467.

52 Budd Hopkins, *Art, Life and UFOs* (San Antonio, TX: Anomalist Books, 2009), 218.

53 Budd Hopkins, *Missing Time* (New York: Ballantine, 1981).

54 The narrative is drawn from both books, but borrows more from *Captured!* than *Interrupted Journey* for several reasons. First, coauthor Kathleen Marden was Betty Hill's niece and experienced many of the family events that happened after the abduction. *Captured!* includes information that was only available after the publication of *Interrupted Journey.* Second, *Captured!* was published long after both Barney and Betty Hill died, making it possible to report details from their hypnosis sessions that John G. Fuller withheld at the request of the Hills and their therapist.

55 I thank Kathleen Marden for her help with this section.

56 The tapes were the joint property of Dr. Simon and the Hills. John G. Fuller had access to some of the tapes when he wrote *Interrupted Journey;* Friedman and Marden had access to all of them when they wrote *Captured!*.

57 Friedman and Marden, *Captured!,* 131.

58 There were discrepancies, but they were minor by comparison to the similarity. See *Captured!,* particularly pp. 115–116.

59 Betty's dream notes are in the appendix of Fuller's *The Interrupted Journey.*

60 Walter Webb, *Encounter at Buff Ledge* (Chicago: CUFOS, 1994).

61 Matthew H. Erdelyi and Joan Becker, "Hypermnesia for Pictures: Incremental Memory for Pictures But Not Words in Multiple Recall Trials" *Cognitive Psychology,* 6(1) (1974), 159–171.

62   Raymond Fowler, *The Allagash Abductions: Undeniable Evidence of Alien Intervention,* 2nd ed. (Columbus, NC: Wildflower Press, 2001).

63   Ron Brown and Don Donderi, "Dream Content and Self-Reported Well-Being Among Recurrent Dreamers, Past-Recurrent Dreamers and Non-recurrent Dreamers," *Journal of Personality and Social Psychology,* 50(3), (1986), 612–623.

64   John S. Carpenter, "Double Abduction Case: Correlation of Hypnosis Data" *Journal of UFO Studies,* New Series, vol. 3 (1991), 91–114.

65   Andrea Pritchard, David E. Pritchard, John E. Mack, Pam Kasey, and Claudia Yapp, eds. *Alien Discussions: Proceedings of the Abduction Study Conference held at MIT, Cambridge, MA* (Cambridge, MA: North Cambridge Press, 1994), 246–253.

66   Budd Hopkins, *Witnessed: The True Story of the Brooklyn Bridge UFO Abductions* (New York: Pocket Books, 1996), 3.

67   Hopkins, *Witnessed,* 310.

68   Hopkins, *Witnessed,* 308–318.

69   Thomas E. Bullard, *The Sympathetic Ear: Investigators as Variables in UFO Abduction Reports* (Mt. Rainier, MD: Fund for UFO Research, 1995).

70   This event sequence is largely based on research by David Jacobs that is included in the Bullard report cited above as well as in Jacobs' own books.

71   Elizabeth Loftus, *Eyewitness Testimony* (Cambridge, MA: Harvard University Press, 1979).

72   "Final Report on the Psychological Testing of UFO 'Abductees'" (Mt. Rainier, MD: Fund for UFO Research, Inc., 1985).

73   Mark Rodeghier, Jeff Goodpaster, and Sandra Blatterbauer, "Psychosocial Characteristics of Abductees: Results from the CUFOS Abduction Project" *Journal of UFO Studies,* New Series vol. 3 (1991), 59–90.

74   Peter Hough and Paul Rogers, "Individuals Who Report Being Abducted by Aliens: Investigating the Differences in Fantasy Proneness, Emotional Intelligence and the Big Five Personality Factors," *Imagination, Cognition and Personality,* vol. 27(2), (2007–2008), 139–161.

75   Nicholas P. Spanos, Cheryl A. Burgess, and Melissa Faith Burgess, "Past-Life Identities, UFO Abductions, and Satanic Ritual Abuse: The Social Construction of Memories," *International Journal of Clinical and Experimental Hypnosis,* vol. 52 (4) (1994), 433–446.

76   Milton H. Erickson and Ernest L. Rossi, *Hypnotherapy: An Exploratory Casebook* (New York: Wiley, 1979).

77   See, for example, Ernest R. Hilgard and Josephine R. Hilgard, *Hypnosis in the Relief of Pain* (Los Altos, CA: William Kaufmann, 1975).

78   Pierre Rainville, Robert K. Hofbauer, Tomás Paus, Gary H. Duncan, M. Catherine Bushnell, and Donald D. Price, "Cerebral Mechanisms of Hypnotic Induction and Suggestion," *Journal of Cognitive Neuroscience,* 11 (1), (1999), 110–125.

79   See, for example, Loftus, *Eyewitness Testimony.*

80   Matthew H. Erdelyi, "Hypermnesia: The Effect of Hypnosis, Fantasy and Concentration," in *Hypnosis and Memory,* Helen M. Pettinati, ed. (New York: Guilford Press, 1988), 64–94.

81   Walter B. Cannon, *Bodily Changes in Pain, Hunger, Fear and Rage* (New York: Appleton, 1929).

82   Marcia Degun-Mather, "Hypnosis in the Treatment of a Case of Dissociative Amnesia for a 12-Year Period" *Contemporary Hypnosis,* vol. 19 (1), (2002), 33–41.

83   See, for example, Amanda J. Barnier, "Posthypnotic Amnesia for Autobiographical Episodes: A Laboratory Model for Functional Amnesia?" *Psychological Science,* vol. 13 (3), (2002), 232–236.

84   Stephen LaBerge, PhD, and Philip G. Zimbardo, PhD, "Event-Related Potential Correlates of Suggested Hypnotic Amnesia," *Sleep and Hypnosis,* vol. 1 (2), (1999), 122–126.

85   For example, Fowler, *The Allagash Abductions,* 49.

86   See for example Budd Hopkins, *Intruders: The Incredible Visitations at Copley Woods* (New York: Random House, 1987). David M. Jacobs, ed., *UFOs and Abductions: Challenging the Borders of Knowledge* (Lawrence, KS: University Press of Kansas, 2000). David M. Jacobs, PhD, *Secret Life: Firsthand Documented Accounts of UFO Abductions* (New York: Simon & Schuster, 1992). Hall, *The UFO Evidence: Volume II.* Clark, *The UFO Encyclopedia,* 2nd ed.

87   See for example Don Donderi, "Response-Contingent Variation in Visual Recall: Evidence of a Dynamic Memory Trace," *Canadian Journal of Psychology,* 44(4), (1990), 423–434. Don Donderi, "Changes in Visual Recall Memory Following Discrimination Learning," *Canadian Journal of Psychology,* vol. 27, (1973) 210–219. and Karim Nader, "New Approaches to Amnesia," *Learning and Memory,* vol. 16 (2009), 672–675.

88   See for example Jacobs, *Secret Life,* 320–326.

89   One exception: David Cherniack's film *UFOs: The Secret History* (Toronto, ON: All-in-One Productions, 2008).

90 Paul R. Hill, *Unconventional Flying Objects* (Charlottesville, VA: Hampton Roads Publishing, 1995). Thank you again Dimitris Hatzopoulos for recommending this very important book to me.

91 Thanks to the intervention of Robert Wood, PhD, who arranged for the publication of the manuscript and wrote the introduction.

92 Hill, *Unconventional Flying Objects,* 107.

93 Ibid., 21.

94 John F. Schuessler, *The Cash-Landrum UFO Incident* (Houston, TX: GeoGraphics Printing, 1988).

95 Robert Salas and James Klotz, *Faded Giant* (n.p.: BookSurge, 2005), 14.

96 Ibid., 14.

97 Ibid., 116.

98 See for example Gardner Murphy and Robert O. Ballou, eds., *William James on Psychical Research* (New York: Viking Press, 1960). J. B. Rhine and J. G. Pratt, *Parapsychology: Frontier Science of the Mind* (Springfield, IL: Charles Thomas, 1957). Sir Hubert Wilkins and Harold M. Sherman, *Thoughts through Space* (New York: Creative Age Press, 1942).

99 Friedman and Marden, *Captured!,* 121.

100 Webb, *Encounter at Buff Ledge,* 12.

101 Fowler, *The Allagash Abductions,* 57.

102 Carpenter, "Double Abduction Case: Correlation of Hypnosis Data," 100.

103 Hopkins, *Witnessed,* 105–107.

104 John Stuart Mill, *A System of Logic,* 8th ed. (New York: Longmans, 1884), 125–126.

105 Albert Einstein, *The Meaning of Relativity,* 6th ed. (London: Methuen, 1956).

106 Alfred North Whitehead, "Laws of Nature" in *Adventures of Ideas* (New York: Macmillan, 1937), 131–151.

107 Whitehead, "Laws of Nature," 129.

108 Albert Einstein, *Ideas and Opinions* (New York: Crown, 1954), 271–272.

109 Thomas Kuhn, *The Structure of Scientific Revolutions,* 2nd ed. (Chicago: University of Chicago Press, 1970), 78–79.

110 Steven Weinberg reminded us that Newtonian mechanics is still both used and understood by students of post-relativity physics in "The Revolution That Didn't Happen," *The New York Review of Books,* vol. XLV, no. 15, 48–52, October 8, 1998.

111 Thomas S. Kuhn, *The Structure of Scientific Revolutions,* 2nd ed., 78–79.

112 Jacobs, *The UFO Controversy in America,* 299–300.

113 Michael Shermer, "UFOs, UAPs and CRAPs," *Scientific American,* April 2011, 90.

114 A clear example of this attitude is expressed by this quote about UFOs from Albert Einstein: "These people have seen something. What it is I do not know and am not curious to know." Einstein, quoted in Jacobs, *The UFO Controversy in America,* 81.

115 See Charles Darwin, *The Voyage of the Beagle,* vol.29 (Cambridge, MA: Harvard Classics, 1909/1845).

116   See Karl Popper, *The Logic of Scientific Discovery* (New York: Harper & Row, 1959), 93–111.

117   William James, *Principles of Psychology*, vol. II (New York: Henry Holt, 1890; Dover publication reprint, 1950), 109.

118   Leon Festinger, *A Theory of Cognitive Dissonance* (Evanston, IL: Row, Peterson, 1957).

119   Sigmund Freud, "The Interpretation of Dreams" in *The Basic Writings of Sigmund Freud,* A. A. Brill, ed. (New York: Random House, 1938), 534–535.

120   Sigmund Freud, "Three Contributions to the Theory of Sex," in *The Basic Writings of Sigmund Freud,* 625–626.

121   Ibid.

122   Philip Morrison, John Billingham, and John Wolfe, eds., *The Search for Extraterrestrial Intelligence* (New York: Dover, 1979).

123   See, for example, *setiathome.berkeley.edu/*

124   There are two "elite scientific culture" exceptions: the *Journal of UFO Studies,* a peer-reviewed scientific journal published by the Center for UFO Studies, which appears irregularly, and the *Journal of Scientific Exploration*, a peer-reviewed scientific journal published by the Society for Scientific Exploration, which appears regularly.

125   Thomas E. Bullard, "UFOs—Folklore of the Space Age," in *UFOs and Popular Culture,* ed. J. R. Lewis (Santa Barbara, CA: ABC-CLIO, 2000), ix–xxv.

126   See, for example, Thomas E. Bullard, "What's New in UFO Abductions? Has the Story Changed in 30 years?" MUFON Symposium Proceedings, 1999, 170–199, and Bullard, "The Sympathetic Ear."

127 Thomas E. Bullard, "Why Abduction Reports Are Not Urban Legends" *International UFO Reporter,* 16(4), (1991), 15–20.

128 J. Allen Hynek, *The UFO Experience: A Scientific Inquiry* (Chicago: Regenery, 1972), 232–233.

129 *www.ufoinfo.com/organizations/index.shtml*

130 *www.nationalarchives.gov.uk/ufos/*

131 *www.ufoevidence.org/topics/russia.htm*

132 See Kean, *UFOs,* and Mark Rodeghier, "Skeptical Failures Down Mexico Way," *International UFO Reporter,* 28(4), (2004), 12.

133 *www.af.mil/information/factsheets/factsheet.asp?id=188*

134 See Richard Dolan, *UFOs and the National Security State* (Charlottesville, VA: Hampton Roads Publishing, 2002), 93.

135 *www.ufoskeptic.org*

136 Thank you, Beth Rogers.

137 Sources differ about the distance from the debris field to the impact site. For example, Carey and Schmitt put it farther from the debris field (Thomas J. Carey and Donald R Schmitt, *Witness to Roswell* [Pompton Plains, NJ: New Page Books, 2009] than Randle and Schmitt do in their earlier book (Kevin D. Randle and Donald R. Schmitt, *UFO Crash at Roswell* [New York: Avon Books, 1991]).

138 Carey and Schmitt, *Witness to Roswell,* 99.

139 Scott Ramsey, Susan Ramsey, Frank Thayer, and Frank Warren's *The Aztec Incident: Recovery at Hart Canyon* (Mooresville, NC: Aztec.48 Productions, 2011) presents evidence that another UFO crashed in northern New Mexico in 1948 and was also secretly recovered by the US government.

140 For example, see Kean, *UFOs,* and Robert L. Hastings, *UFOs and Nukes* (Bloomington, IN: Authorhouse, 2008).

141 Kean, *UFOs,* 222–229.

142 See also Clark, *The UFO Encyclopedia.*

143 Alexander Wendt and Raymond Duvall, "Sovereignty and the UFO," *Political Theory,* vol. 16(4), (2008), 607–633. See also Alexander Wendt and Raymond Duvall, "Militant Agnosticism and the UFO Taboo" in Kean, *UFOs,* 269–281.

144 Miguel Leon-Portilla, *The Broken Spears: The Aztec Account of the Conquest of Mexico* (Boston: Beacon Press, 1990).

145 *www.af.mil/information/factsheets/factsheet.asp?fsID=188*

146 See Donald R. Burleson, "UFO Secrecy and the Law," *International UFO Reporter,* vol. 28 (4), (2004), 14–18.

147 *www.ufoskeptic.org/*

148 A minor misquote. Lovell, mission commander, actually said "Houston, we've had a problem." But the misquote went into the film and it is much snappier.
See *www.phrases.org.uk*

149 H. A. L. Fisher, *A History of Europe,* vol. I: Ancient and Medieval (London: Eyre and Spottiswoode, 1935), vii.

Selected Readings

This is a list of publications that I have found useful. There are books, magazines and journals, videos, and websites. Books that are a good starting point for someone who knows little and wants to learn more about UFOs and extraterrestrials are in **bold**.

Books and Articles

Bryan, C. D. B. *Close Encounters of the Fourth Kind.* New York: Knopf, 1995.

Clancy, Susan A. *Abducted: How People Come to Believe They Were Kidnapped by Aliens.* Cambridge, MA: Harvard University Press, 2005.

Clark, Jerome. *The UFO Encyclopedia: The Phenomenon from the Beginning.* Detroit, MI: Omnigraphics, 1998.

Condon, Dr. Edward U. *Scientific Study of Unidentified Flying Objects* (the Condon Committee Report). New York: Bantam Press, 1969.

Dolan, Richard M. *UFOs and the National Security State: Chronology of a Cover-Up, 1941–1973.* Charlottesville, VA: Hampton Roads, 2002.

Fowler, Raymond E. *The Allagash Abductions: Undeniable Evidence of Alien Intervention,* 2nd ed. Columbus, NC: Wild Flower Press, 1993.

Friedman, Stanton T., and Don Berliner. *Crash at Corona: The U.S. Military Retrieval and Cover-Up of a UFO.* New York: Paragon House, 1992.

Friedman, Stanton T., and Kathleen Marden. *Captured! The Betty and Barney Hill UFO Experience: The True Story of the World's First Documented Alien Abduction.* Franklin Lakes, NJ: New Page Books, 2007.

Fuller, John G. *Incident at Exeter: Unidentified Flying Objects Over America Now.* New York: Putnam, 1966.

————. *The Interrupted Journey: Two Lost Hours "Aboard a Flying Saucer."* New York: Dial Press, 1966.

Hall, Richard H. *The UFO Evidence, Volume II: A Thirty-Year Report.* Oxford, UK: Scarecrow Press, 2001.

Hastings, Robert. *UFOs and Nukes: Extraordinary Encounters at Nuclear Weapons Sites.* Bloomington, IN: Author House, 2008.

Hill, Paul R. *Unconventional Flying Objects: A Scientific Analysis.* Charlottesville, VA: Hampton Roads, 1995.

Hopkins, Budd. *Missing Time.* New York: Ballantine Books, 1988.

————. *Intruders: The Incredible Visitations at Copley Woods.* New York: Ballantine, 1987.

————. **Witnessed: The True Story of the Brooklyn Bridge UFO Abductions.** New York: Pocket Books, 1996.

Hynek, J. Allen. *The UFO Experience: A Scientific Inquiry.* Chicago: Henry Regenery Co., 1972.

Hynek, J. Allen, Philip J. Imbrogno, and Bob Pratt. *Night Siege: The Hudson Valley UFO Sightings,* 2nd ed. St. Paul, MN: Llewellyn Publications, 1998.

Hynek, J. Allen, et. al. *Symposium on Unidentified Flying Objects: Hearings Before the Committee on Science and Astronautics, U.S. House of Representatives, Ninetieth Congress, Second Session {No. 7}.* Washington, DC: US Government Printing Office, 1968.

Jacobs, David M. *The UFO Controversy in America.* Bloomington, IN: Indiana University Press, 1975.

Jacobs, David M., ed. *UFOs and Abductions: Challenging the Borders of Science.* Lawrence, KS: University Press of Kansas, 2000.

Jacobs, David M., PhD. *Secret Life: Firsthand Accounts of UFO Abductions.* New York: Simon & Schuster, 1992.

———. *The Threat: Revealing the Secret Alien Agenda.* New York: Simon & Schuster, 1998.

Jung, C. G. *Flying Saucers: A Modern Myth of Things Seen in the Sky.* Translated by R. F. C. Hull. New York: MJF Books, 1978.

Kean, Leslie. *UFOs: Generals, Pilots, and Government Officials Go on the Record.* New York: Harmony Books, 2010.

Klass, Philip J. *UFO Abduction: A Dangerous Game.* Buffalo, NY: Prometheus Books, 1989.

Lewis, James R. *UFOs and Popular Culture: An Encyclopedia of Contemporary Myth.* Santa Barbara, CA: ABC-CLIO, 2000.

Menzel, Donald H. *The World of Flying Saucers: A Scientific Examination of a Major Myth of the Space Age.* New York: Doubleday, 1963.

Pritchard, Andrea, David E. Pritchard, John E. Mack, Pam Kasey, and Claudia Yapp, eds. *Alien Discussions: Proceedings of the Abduction Study Conference Held at MIT, Cambridge, MA.* Cambridge, MA: North Cambridge Press, 1994.

Randle, Kevin D., and Donald R. Schmitt. *UFO Crash at Roswell.* New York: Avon Books, 1991.

Ruppelt, Edward J. *The Report on Unidentified Flying Objects.* New York: Ace Books, 1956.

Salas, Robert, and James Klotz. *Faded Giant: The 1967 Missile/ UFO Incidents.* BookSurge, LLC, 2005.

Schuessler, John F. *The Cash-Landrum Incident.* LaPorte, TX: Geo Graphics, 1998.

Sagan, Carl, and Thornton Page, eds. *UFO's: A Scientific Debate.* New York: Barnes & Noble, 1972.

Sturrock, Peter A. *The UFO Enigma: A New Review of the Physical Evidence.* New York: Warner Books, 1999.

Vallée, Jacques. *Anatomy of a Phenomenon.* New York: Ace Books, 1965.

Webb, Walter N. *Encounter at Buff Ledge: A UFO Case History.* Chicago: Center for UFO Studies, 1994.

Video

Barker, Darryl. *The Edge of Reality: Illinois UFO, January 5, 2000.* Darryl Barker Productions, 2001.

Cherniack, David. *UFOs: The Secret History.* UFOTV.com catalog no. U8698, 2008.

Journals and Magazines

Journal of Scientific Exploration. Lawrence, KS: Allen Press.

MUFON UFO Journal. Fort Collins, CO: Mutual UFO Network.

Websites

Bernard Haisch (former editor, *Astrophysical Journal* and *Journal of Scientific Exploration*): *www.ufoskeptic.org*

British UFO Research Association: *www.bufora.org.uk*

Center for UFO Studies (CUFOS): *www.cufos.org*

Centre National des Études Spatiaux: *www.cnes-geipan.fr/geipan*

Committee for the Scientific Investigation of Claims of the Paranormal *www.csicop.org*

Fund for UFO Research (FUFOR): *www.fufor.com*

Mutual UFO Network (MUFON): *www.mufon.com*

United Kingdom Ministry of Defence: *www.nationalarchives.gov.uk/ufos*

Index

S

Sagan, Carl, 49, 59, 62–63, 218

Salas, Robert, 155, 218

Saturday Review, 55

saucer patrol, 5

scars, 127, 129

Shermer, Michael, 163–164

Schmitt, Donald R., 181–184, 200, 218

Schuessler, John F., 200, 218

Schulze, Glen, 70

Science in Default, 60

Science magazine, 58, 61, 169

Scientific American magazine, 163

scientific revolutions, 162, 165

Search for Extraterrestrial Intelligence (SETI), 49, 169

Selective Service Act, 192

Sharkey, Douglas, 107–108

Sillard, Yves, 81

Simon, Benjamin, 93–94, 97–98, 105, 140

Skeptic magazine, 163

Skeptics, xiii, 5, 59, 62, 130–131, 134, 199

Slater, Elizabeth, 132–134, 143

Smith, Jim, xi–xiv

Socorro, New Mexico case, 41–42

South Korea, 17

Soviet Union, 3, 15–17, 26

sperm sample, 114

Stalin, Joseph, 17

standard model, 78

star map, 96, 99

Stephenville, Texas, 70

Stonehenge Apartments, 84

strangeness-probability (S-P) diagram, 59

Structure of Scientific Revolutions, The, 162

Sublimation, 168

swamp gas, 43, 58

Swords, Michael, 199

System of Logic, 159

T

Taconic State Parkway sightings, ix, xii, 63–66, 68, 71, 150

Telepathy, 156

temperature inversions, 24–25, 163

Thematic Apperception Test (TAT), 132

Thucydides, 20

top secret, 22, 174

Topeka, Kansas, 7

Tossie, Guy, 78–80, 85, 90

Touchstone, 52–53, 70, 102–103, 109, 125, 126, 141

Truman, Harry S., 24–25, 44, 184, 187–188

U

West Nyack, New York case,
107–110, 127, 141
Westrum, Ron, 199
Whitehead, Alfred North, 160
Wright-Patterson Air Force Base,
14, 26, 60, 179–180, 183–184

Y, Z

Yukon Territory event, 68–70
Zamora, Lonnie, 41–42, 90
Zeiss Ultraphot III microscope
system, xv
Zeta 1 and Zeta 2 Reticuli, 99

About the Author

DON DONDERI is a citizen of both the US and Canada. He entered the University of Chicago at age 15, and graduated with a BA and BSC in biological psychology at age 21. He worked as an applied psychologist for IBM Corporation, developing navigation displays for the B-52 bomber. He served as Associate Dean of the Faculty of Graduate Studies and Research at McGill University.

Hampton Roads Publishing Company
. . . for the evolving human spirit

Hampton Roads Publishing Company publishes books on a variety
of subjects, including spirituality, health, and other related topics.

For a copy of our latest trade catalog, call (978) 465-0504 or visit
our distributor's website at *www.redwheelweiser.com.* You can also
sign up for our newsletter and special offers by going to
www.redwheelweiser.com/newsletter/.